Kate Douglas Smith Wiggin

A Cathedral Courtship and Penelope's English Experiences

Kate Douglas Smith Wiggin

A Cathedral Courtship and Penelope's English Experiences

ISBN/EAN: 9783337339005

Printed in Europe, USA, Canada, Australia, Japan

Cover: Foto ©Thomas Meinert / pixelio.de

More available books at **www.hansebooks.com**

A CATHEDRAL COURTSHIP

AND PENELOPE'S ENGLISH EXPERIENCES

BY

KATE DOUGLAS WIGGIN

WITH FIVE ILLUSTRATIONS
BY CLIFFORD CARLETON

BOSTON AND NEW YORK
HOUGHTON, MIFFLIN AND
COMPANY.   M DCCC XCIII

TO MY BOSTON FRIEND

SALEMINA

NO ANGLOMANIAC, BUT

A TRUE BRITON

CONTENTS

LIST OF ILLUSTRATIONS

A CATHEDRAL COURTSHIP

WINCHESTER, *May* 28, 1891.
The Royal Garden Inn.

WE are doing the English cathedral towns, aunt Celia and I. Aunt Celia has an intense desire to improve my mind. Papa told her, when we were leaving Cedarhurst, that he would n't for the world have it too much improved, and aunt Celia remarked that, so far as she could judge, there was no immediate danger; with which exchange of hostilities they parted.

We are traveling under the yoke of an iron itinerary, warranted neither to bend nor break. It was made out by a young High Church curate in New York, and if it had been blessed by all the bishops and

popes it could not be more sacred to aunt
Celia.   She is awfully High Church, and
I believe she thinks this tour of the cathedrals will give me a taste for ritual and
bring me into the true fold.   I have been
hearing dear old Dr. Kyle a great deal
lately, and aunt Celia says that he is the
most dangerous Unitarian she knows,
because he has leanings towards Chris-
tianity.

Long ago, in her youth, she was engaged to a young architect.   He, with his
triangles and T-squares and things, succeeded in making an imaginary scale-draw-
ing of her heart (up to that time a virgin
forest, an unmapped territory), which en-
abled him to enter in and set up a pedes-
tal there, on which he has remained ever
since.   He has been only a memory for
many years, to be sure, for he died at the
age of twenty-six, before he had had time
to build anything but a livery stable and
a country hotel.   This is fortunate, on the
whole, because aunt Celia thinks he was
destined to establish American architecture on a higher plane, — rid it of its base,
time-serving, imitative instincts, and waft

it to a height where, in the course of centuries, we should have been revered and
followed by all the nations of the earth.
I went to see the livery stable, after one
of these Miriam-like flights of prophecy on
the might-have-been. It is n't fair to judge
a man's promise by one performance, and
that one a livery stable, so I shall say
nothing.

This sentiment about architecture and
this fondness for the very toppingest High
Church ritual cause aunt Celia to look
on the English cathedrals with solemnity
and reverential awe. She has given me
a fat notebook, with " Katharine Schuyler" stamped in gold letters on the Rus-
sia leather cover, and a lock and key to
protect its feminine confidences. I am
not at all the sort of girl who makes notes,
and I have told her so; but she says that
I must at least record my passing impressions, if they are ever so trivial and com-
monplace.

I wanted to go directly from Southampton to London with the Abbotts, our ship
friends, who left us yesterday. Roderick
Abbott and I had had a charming time on

board ship (more charming than aunt
Celia knows, because she was very ill, and
her natural powers of chaperoning were
severely impaired), and the prospect of
seeing London sights together was not un-
pleasing ; but Roderick Abbott is not in
aunt Celia's itinerary, which reads : " Winchester, Salisbury, Wells, Bath, Bristol,
Gloucester, Oxford, London, Ely, Lincoln,
York, Durham."

Aunt Celia is one of those persons who
are born to command, and when they are
thrown in contact with those who are born
to be commanded all goes as merry as a
marriage bell ; otherwise not.

So here we are at Winchester ; and I
don't mind all the Roderick Abbotts in the
universe, now that I have seen the Royal
Garden Inn, its pretty coffee-room opening
into the old-fashioned garden, with its
borders of clove pinks, its aviaries, and its
blossoming horse-chestnuts, great towering masses of pink bloom !

Aunt Celia has driven to St. Cross
Hospital with Mrs. Benedict, an estimable
lady tourist whom she " picked up " *en
route* from Southampton.   I am tired, and

stayed at home. I cannot write letters, because aunt Celia has the guide-books, so I sit by the window in indolent content, watching the dear little school laddies, with their short jackets and wide white collars; they all look so jolly, and rosy, and clean, and kissable! I should like to kiss the chambermaid, too! She has a pink print dress; no bangs, thank goodness (it 's curious our servants can't leave that deformity to the upper classes), but shining brown hair, plump figure, soft voice, and a most engaging way of saying, "Yes, miss? Anythink more, miss?" I long to ask her to sit down comfortably and be English. while I study her as a type, but of course I must n't. Sometimes I wish I could retire from the world for a season and do what I like, "surrounded by the general comfort of being thought mad."

An elegant, irreproachable, high-minded model of dignity and reserve has just knocked and inquired what we will have for dinner. It is very embarrassing to give orders to a person who looks like a judge of the Supreme Court, but I said languidly, "What would you suggest?"

"How would you like a clear soup, a good spring soup, to begin with, miss?"

"Very much."

"And a bit of turbot next, miss?"

"Yes, turbot, by all means," I said, my mouth watering at the word.

"And what for a roast, miss? Would you enjoy a young duckling, miss?"

"Just the thing; and for dessert"— I could n't think what we ought to have for dessert in England, but the high-minded model coughed apologetically and said, "I was thinking you might like gooseberry tart and cream for a sweet, miss."

Oh that I could have vented my New World enthusiasm in a shriek of delight as I heard those intoxicating words, heretofore met only in English novels!

"Ye-es," I said hesitatingly, though I was palpitating with joy, "I fancy we should like gooseberry tart" (here a bright idea entered my mind); "and perhaps in case my aunt does n't care for the gooseberry tart, you might bring a lemon squash, please."

Now I had never met a lemon squash personally, but I had often heard of it, and wished to show my familiarity with British culinary art.

"One lemon squash, miss?"

"Oh, as to that, it does n't matter," I said haughtily; "bring a sufficient number for two persons."

.   .   .   .

Aunt Celia came home in the highest feather. She had twice been taken for an Englishwoman. She said she thought that lemon squash was a drink; I thought it was a pie; but we shall find out at dinner, for, as I said, I ordered a sufficient number for two persons.

At four o'clock we attended even-song at the cathedral. I shall not say what I felt when the white-surpliced boy choir entered, winding down those vaulted aisles, or when I heard for the first time that intoned service, with all its "witchcraft of harmonic sound." I sat quite by myself in a high carved-oak seat, and the hour was passed in a trance of serene delight. I do not have many opinions, it is true, but papa says I am always strong on sentiments; nevertheless, I shall not attempt to tell even what I feel in these new and

beautiful experiences, for it has been better told a thousand times.

There were a great many people at service, and a large number of Americans
among them, I should think, though we
saw no familiar faces. There was one
particularly nice young man, who looked
like a Bostonian. He sat opposite me.
He did n't stare, — he was too well bred;
but when I looked the other way, he looked
at me. Of course I could feel his eyes, —
anybody can, at least any girl can; but I
attended to every word of the service, and
was as good as an angel. When the procession had filed out and the last strain of
the great organ had rumbled into silence,
we went on a tour through the cathedral,
a heterogeneous band, headed by a conscientious old verger who did his best to
enlighten us, and succeeded in virtually
spoiling my pleasure.

After we had finished (think of " finish-
ing " a cathedral in an hour or two !), aunt
Celia and I, with one or two others, wandered through the beautiful close, looking
at the exterior from every possible point,
and coming at last to a certain ruined arch

which is very famous. It did not strike
me as being remarkable. I could make
any number of them with a pattern, without the least effort. But at any rate,
when told by the verger to gaze upon the
beauties of this wonderful relic and tremble,
we were obliged to gaze also upon the
beauties of the aforesaid nice young man,
who was sketching it. As we turned to
go away, aunt Celia dropped her bag. It
is one of those detestable, all-absorbing,
all-devouring, thoroughly respectable, but
never proud Boston bags, made of black
cloth with leather trimmings, "C. Van T."
embroidered on the side, and the top
drawn up with stout cords which pass over
the Boston wrist or arm. As for me, I
loathe them, and would not for worlds be
seen carrying one, though I do slip a great
many necessaries into aunt Celia's.

I hastened to pick up the horrid thing,
for fear the nice young man would feel
obliged to do it for me; but, in my inde-
corous haste, I caught hold of the wrong
end and emptied the entire contents on
the stone flagging. Aunt Celia did n't
notice; she had turned with the verger,

lest she should miss a single word of his inspired testimony. So we scrambled up the articles together, the nice young man and I ; and oh, I hope I may never look upon his face again !

There were prayer-books and guide-books, a bottle of soda mint tablets, a spool of dental floss, a Bath bun, a bit of gray frizz that aunt Celia pins into her steamer cap, a spectacle case, a brandy flask, and a bonbon box, which broke and scattered cloves and cardamom seeds. (I hope he guessed aunt Celia is a dyspeptic, and not intemperate !) All this was hopelessly vulgar, but I would n't have minded anything if there had not been a Duchess novel. Of course he thought that it belonged to me. He could n't have known aunt Celia was carrying it for that accidental Mrs. Benedict, with whom she went to St. Cross Hospital.

After scooping the cardamom seeds out of the cracks in the stone flagging, he handed me the tattered, disreputable-looking copy of " A Modern Circe " with a bow that would n't have disgraced a Chester-

" We scrambled up tne articles together "

a

field, and then went back to his easel, while I fled after aunt Celia and her verger.

.   .   .   .

Memoranda : *The Winchester Cathedral has the longest nave. The inside is more superb than the outside. Izaak Walton and Jane Austen are buried there.*

HE

WINCHESTER, *May* 28, 1891.
The White Swan.

As sure as my name is Jack Copley, I saw the prettiest girl in the world to-day, — an American, too, or I 'm greatly mistaken. It was in the cathedral, where I have been sketching for several days. I was sitting in the end of a seat, at afternoon service, when two ladies entered by the side door. The ancient maiden, evidently the head of the family, settled herself devoutly, and the young one stole off by herself to one of the old carved seats back of the choir. She was worse than pretty! I took a sketch of her during service, as she sat under the dark carved-oak canopy, with this Latin inscription over her head : —

CARLTON CUM
DOLBY
LETANIA
IX SOLIDORUM
SUPER FLUMINA
CONFITEBOR TIBI
DŪC PROBATI

There ought to be a law against a woman's making a picture of herself, unless she is willing to sit and be sketched.

A black and white sketch does n't give any definite idea of this charmer's charms, but some time I 'll fill it in, — hair, sweet little hat, gown, and eyes, all in golden brown, a cape of tawny sable slipping off her arm, a knot of yellow primroses in her girdle, carved-oak background, and the afternoon sun coming through a stained-glass window. Great Jove! She had a most curious effect on me, that girl! I can't explain it, — very curious, altogether new, and rather pleasant! When one of the choir boys sang, "Oh for the wings of a dove!" a tear rolled out of one of her lovely eyes and down her smooth brown cheek. I would have given a large portion of my modest monthly income for the felicity of wiping away that teardrop with one of my new handkerchiefs, marked with a tremendous " C " by my pretty sister.

An hour or two later they appeared again, — the dragon, who answers to the name of "aunt Celia," and the "nut-brown mayde," who comes when you call her " Katharine." I was sketching a ruined arch. The dragon dropped her unmistakably Boston bag. I expected to see encyclopædias and Russian tracts fall from it, but was disappointed. The nut-brown mayde (who has been brought up rigidly) hastened to pick up the bag, for fear that I should serve her by doing it. She was punished by turning it inside out, and I was rewarded by helping her pick up the articles, which were many and ill assorted. My little romance received the first blow when I found that she reads the Duchess novels. I think, however, she has the grace to be ashamed of it, for she blushed scarlet when I handed her " A Modern Circe." I could have told her that such a blush on such a cheek would atone for reading Mrs. Southworth, but I refrained. After she had gone I discovered a slip of paper which had blown under some stones. It proved to be an itinerary. I did n't return it. I thought they must know which way they were going; and as this was precisely what I wanted to know, I kept it for my own use. She is doing the cathedral towns. I am doing the cathedral towns. Happy thought! Why should n't we do them together, — we and aunt Celia?

I had only ten minutes to catch my train for Salisbury, but I concluded to run in and glance at the registers of the principal hotels. Found my nut-brown mayde at once on the pages of the Royal Garden Inn register: "Miss Celia Van Tyck, Beverly, Mass.; Miss Katharine Schuyler, New York." I concluded to stay over another train, ordered dinner, and took an altogether indefensible and inconsistent pleasure in writing "John Quincy Copley, Cambridge, Mass.," directly beneath the charmer's autograph.

· · · · · · · ·

SALISBURY, *June* 1.
The White Hart Inn.

We left Winchester on the 1.06 train
yesterday, and here we are within sight of
another superb and ancient pile of stone.
I wanted so much to stop at the Highflyer
Inn in Lark Lane, but aunt Celia said
that if we were destitute of personal dignity, we at least owed something to our
ancestors. Aunt Celia has a tempera-
mental distrust of joy as something dangerous and ensnaring. She does n't realize what fun it would be to date one's
letters from the Highflyer Inn, Lark Lane,
even if one were obliged to consort with
poachers and cockneys in order to do it.

We attended service at three. The
music was lovely, and there were beautiful stained-glass windows by Burne-Jones
and Morris. The verger (when wound up
with a shilling) talked like an electric doll.
If that nice young man is making a cathedral tour, like ourselves, he is n't taking our route, for he is n't here. If he has
come over for the purpose of sketching,

he would n't stop at sketching one cathedral. Perhaps he began at the other end
and worked down to Winchester. Yes,
that must be it, for the Ems sailed yesterday from Southampton.

.   .   .   .

June 2.

We intended to go to Stonehenge this
morning, but it rained, so we took a
" growler " and went to the Earl of Pem-
broke's country place to see the pictures.
Had a delightful morning with the magnificent antiques, curios, and portraits. The
Van Dyck room is a joy forever. There
were other visitors ; nobody who looked
especially interesting. Don't like Salisbury so well as Winchester. Don't know
why. We shall drive this afternoon, if it
is fair, and go to Wells to-morrow. Must
read Baedeker on the bishop's palace.
Oh dear ! if one could only have a good
time and not try to know anything !

Memoranda : *This cathedral has the
highest spire. Remember : Winchester,
longest nave ; Salisbury, highest spire.*

*The Lancet style is those curved lines
meeting in a rounding or a sharp point like*

this ⌒ ⌒ *and then joined together like*
this ⌄⌄⌄ *the way they used*
to scallop flannel petticoats. Gothic looks
like triangles meeting together in various
spots and joined with beautiful sort of orna-
mented knobs. I think I know Gothic when
I see it. Then there is Norman, Early
English, fully developed Early English,
Early and Late Perpendicular, and Transi-
tion. Aunt Celia knows them all apart.

HE

SALISBURY, *June* 3.
The Red Lion.

I went off on a long tramp this afternoon, and coming on a pretty river flow-
ing through green meadows, with a fringe
of trees on either side, I sat down to
make a sketch. I heard feminine voices
in the vicinity, but, as these are generally
a part of the landscape in the tourist season, I paid no special notice. Suddenly
a dainty patent-leather shoe floated towards me on the surface of the stream.
It evidently had just dropped in, for it
was right side up with care, and was dis-

porting itself right merrily. "Did ever
Jove's tree drop such fruit?" I quoted,
as I fished it out on my stick ; and just
then I heard a distressed voice saying,
"Oh, aunt Celia, I 've lost my smart little
London shoe.   I was sitting in a tree,
taking a pebble out of the heel, when I
saw a caterpillar, and I dropped it into
the river, the shoe, you know, not the caterpillar."   Hereupon she came in sight, and
I witnessed the somewhat unusual spectacle of my nut-brown mayde hopping on
one foot, like a divine stork, and ever and
anon emitting a feminine shriek as her
off foot, clad in a delicate silk stocking,
came in contact with the ground.   I rose
quickly, and, polishing the patent leather
ostentatiously, inside and out, with my
handkerchief, I offered it to her with
distinguished grace.   She swayed on her
one foot with as much dignity as possible,
and then recognizing me as the person
who picked up the contents of aunt Celia's bag, she said, dimpling in the most
distracting manner (that 's another thing
there ought to be a law against), "Thank
you again ; you seem to be a sort of
knight-errant!"

"Shall I — assist you?" I asked. (I might have known that this was going too far.)

"No, thank you," she said, with polar frigidity. "Good-afternoon." And she hopped back to her aunt Celia without another word.

I don't know how to approach aunt Celia. She is formidable. By a curious accident of feature, for which she is not in the least responsible, she always wears an unfortunate expression as of one perceiving some offensive odor in the immediate vicinity. This may be a mere accident of high birth. It is the kind of nose often seen in the "first families," and her name betrays the fact that she is of good old Knickerbocker origin. We go to Wells to-morrow. At least I think we do.

SHE

GLOUCESTER, *June* 9.
The Spread Eagle.

I met him at Wells, and again at Bath. We are always being ridiculous, and he is always rescuing us. Aunt Celia never really sees him, and thus never recognizes him when he appears again, always as the flower of chivalry and guardian of ladies in distress.   I will never again travel abroad without a man, even if I have to hire one from a Feeble-Minded Asylum. We work like galley slaves, aunt Celia and I, finding out about trains and things. Neither of us can understand Bradshaw, and I can't even grapple with the lesser intricacies of the A B C railway guide. The trains, so far as I can see, always arrive before they go out, and I can never tell whether to read up the page or down. It is certainly very queer that the stupid-est man that breathes, one that barely escapes idiocy, can disentangle a railway guide, when the brightest woman fails. Even the Boots at the inn in Wells took my book, and, rubbing his frightfully dirty finger down the row of puzzling figures, found the place in a minute, and said, "There ye are, miss."   It is very humili-ating.   All the time I have left from the study of routes and hotels I spend on guide-books.   Now I 'm sure that if any one of the men I know were here, he could tell me all that is necessary as we walk along the streets. I don't say it in a frivolous or sentimental spirit in the least, but I do affirm that there is hardly any juncture in life where one is n't better off for having a man about. I should never dare divulge this to aunt Celia, for she does n't think men very nice. She excludes them from conversation as if they were indelicate subjects.

But, to go on, we were standing at the door of Ye Olde Bell and Horns, at Bath, waiting for the fly which we had ordered to take us to the station, when who should drive up in a four-wheeler but the flower of chivalry. Aunt Celia was saying very audibly, " We shall certainly miss the train if the man does n't come at once."

" Pray take this fly," said the flower of chivalry. " I am not leaving till the next train."

Aunt Celia got in without a murmur; I sneaked in after her. I don't think she looked at him, though she did vouchsafe the remark that he seemed to be a civil sort of person.

At Bristol, I was walking about by my-

self, and I espied a sign, " Martha Huggins, Licensed Victualer." It was a nice,
tidy little shop, with a fire on the hearth
and flowers in the window, and, as it was
raining smartly, I thought no one would
catch me if I stepped inside to chat with
Martha. I fancied it would be so delightful and Dickensy to talk quietly with a
licensed victualer by the name of Martha
Huggins.

Just after I had settled myself, the flower
of chivalry came in and ordered ale. I
was disconcerted at being found in a
dramshop alone, for I thought, after the
bag episode, he might fancy us a family
of inebriates. But he did n't evince the
slightest astonishment ; he merely lifted
his hat, and walked out after he had finished his ale. He certainly has the love-
liest manners !

And so it goes on, and we never get any
further. I like his politeness and his evi-
dent feeling that I can't be flirted and
talked with like a forward boarding-school
miss, but I must say I don't think much
of his ingenuity. Of course one can't have
all the virtues, but, if I were he, I would

part with my distinguished air, my charming ease, in fact almost anything, if I could have in exchange a few grains of common sense, just enough to guide me in the practical affairs of life.

I wonder what he is? He might be an artist, but he does n't seem quite like an artist; or a dilettante, but he does n't seem in the least like a dilettante. Or he might be an architect; I think that is the most probable guess of all. Perhaps he is only "going to be" one of these things, for he can't be more than twenty-five or twenty-six. Still he looks as if he were something already; that is, he has a kind of self-reliance in his mien, — not self-assertion, nor self-esteem, but belief in self, as if he were able, and knew that he was able, to conquer circumstances.

. . . .

HE

GLOUCESTER, *June* 10.
The Bell.

Nothing accomplished yet. Her aunt is a Van Tyck, and a stiff one, too. I am

a Copley, and that delays matters. Much
depends upon the manner of approach.
A false move would be fatal. We have
six more towns (as per itinerary), and if
their thirst for cathedrals is n't slaked
when these are finished we have the entire
continent to do. If I could only succeed
in making an impression on the retina of
aunt Celia's eye! Though I have been
under her feet for ten days, she never yet
has observed me. This absent-minded-
ness of hers serves me ill now, but it may
prove a blessing later on.

. . . .

SHE

OXFORD, *June* 12.
The Mitre.

It was here in Oxford that a grain of
common sense entered the brain of the
flower of chivalry. You might call it the
dawn of reason. We had spent part of
the morning in High Street, "the noblest
old street in England," as our dear Hawthorne calls it. As Wordsworth had written a sonnet about it, aunt Celia was

armed for the fray, —a volume of Wordsworth in one hand, and one of Hawthorne
in the other. (I wish Baedeker did n't
give such full information about what one
ought to read before one can approach
these places in a proper spirit.) When
we had done High Street, we went to
Magdalen College, and sat down on a
bench in Addison's Walk, where aunt
Celia proceeded to store my mind with
the principal facts of Addison's career,
and his influence on the literature of the
something or other century. The cram-
ming process over, we wandered along,
and came upon " him " sketching a shady
corner of the walk.

Aunt Celia went up behind him, and,
Van Tyck though she is, she could not
restrain her admiration of his work. I
was surprised myself : I did n't suppose
so good looking a youth could do such
good work. I retired to a safe distance,
and they chatted together. He offered
her the sketch; she refused to take advantage of his kindness. He said he
would "dash off" another that evening,
and bring it to our hotel, — "so glad to

do anything for a fellow-countryman," etc.
I peeped from behind a tree and saw him
give her his card. It was an awful moment ; I trembled, but she read it with
unmistakable approval, and gave him her
own with an expression that meant, " Yours
is good, but beat that if you can ! "

She called to me, and I appeared. Mr.
John Quincy Copley, Cambridge, was
presented to her niece, Miss Katharine
Schuyler, New York. It was over, and a
very small thing to take so long about,
too.

He is an architect, and of course has a
smooth path into aunt Celia's affections.
Theological students, ministers, mission-
aries, heroes, and martyrs she may distrust, but architects never !

" He is an architect, my dear Katharine, and he is a Copley," she told me
afterwards. " I never knew a Copley who
was not respectable, and many of them
have been more."

After the introduction was over, aunt
Celia asked him guilelessly if he had
visited any other of the English cathedrals.
Any others, indeed ! This to a youth

who had been all but in her lap for a fortnight ! It was a blow, but he rallied bravely, and, with an amused look in my direction, replied discreetly that he had visited most of them at one time or another. I refused to let him see that I had ever noticed him before ; that is, particularly.

. . . .

Memoranda : " *The very stones and mortar of this historic town seem impregnated with the spirit of restful antiquity.*" (Extract from one of aunt Celia's letters.) *Among the great men who have studied here are the Prince of Wales, Duke of Wellington, Gladstone, Sir Robert Peel, Sir Philip Sidney, William Penn, John Locke, the two Wesleys, Ruskin, Ben Jonson, and Thomas Otway.* (Look Otway up.)

HE

OXFORD, *June* 13.
The Angel.

I have done it, and if I had n't been a fool and a coward, I might have done it a week ago, and spared myself a good deal of delicious torment.   I have just given two hours to a sketch of Addison's Walk and carried it to aunt Celia at the Mitre. Object, to find out whether they make a long stay in London (our next point), and if so where.   It seems they go directly through.   I said in the course of conversation, " So Miss Schuyler is willing to forego a London season ? Marvelous self-denial ! "

"My niece did not come to Europe for a London season," replied Miss Van Tyck. "We go through London this time merely as a cathedral town, simply because it chances to be where it is geographically. We shall visit St. Paul's and Westminster Abbey, and then go directly on, that our chain of impressions may have absolute continuity and be free from any disturbing elements."

Oh, but she is lovely, is aunt Celia !

.   .   .   .

LINCOLN, *June* 20.
The Black Boy Inn.

I am stopping at a beastly little hole, which has the one merit of being opposite Miss Schuyler's lodgings. My sketch-book has deteriorated in artistic value during the last two weeks. Many of its pages, while interesting to me as reminiscences, will hardly do for family or studio exhibition. If I should label them, the result would be something like this : —

1. Sketch of a footstool and desk where I first saw Miss Schuyler kneeling.

2. Sketch of a carved-oak chair, Miss Schuyler sitting in it.

3. "Angel Choir." Heads of Miss Schuyler introduced into the carving.

4. Altar screen. Full length figure of Miss Schuyler holding lilies.

5. Tomb of a bishop, where I tied Miss Schuyler's shoe.

6. Tomb of another bishop, where I had to tie it again because I did it so badly the first time.

7. Sketch of the shoe ; the shoe-lace worn out with much tying.

8. Sketch of the blessed verger who called her " madam," when we were walking together.

9. Sketch of her blush when he did it ; the prettiest thing in the world.

10. Sketch of J. Q. Copley contemplating the ruins of his heart.

" How are the mighty fallen ! "

.   .   .   .

SHE

LINCOLN, *June* 22.
At Miss Brown's, Castle Garden.

Mr. Copley *has* done something in the world ; I was sure that he had. He has a little income of his own, but he is too proud and ambitious to be an idler. He looked so manly when he talked about it, standing up straight and strong in his knickerbockers. I like men in knickerbockers. Aunt Celia does n't. She says she does n't see how a well-brought-up Copley can go about with his legs in that condition. I would give worlds to know how aunt Celia ever unbent sufficiently to get engaged. But, as I was saying, Mr.

Copley has accomplished something, young
as he is. He has built three picturesque
suburban churches suitable for weddings,
and a state lunatic asylum.

Aunt Celia says we shall have no worthy
architecture until every building is made
an exquisitely sincere representation of its
deepest purpose, — a symbol, as it were,
of its indwelling meaning. I should think
it would be very difficult to design a lunatic asylum on that basis, but I did n't dare
say so, as Mr. Copley seemed to think it all
right. Their conversation is absolutely
sublimated when they get to talking of
architecture. I have just copied two quotations from Emerson, and am studying
them every night for fifteen minutes before
I go to sleep. I 'm going to quote them
some time offhand, just after morning service, when we are wandering about the cathedral grounds. The first is this : " The
Gothic cathedral is a blossoming in stone,
subdued by the insatiable demand of harmony in man. The mountain of granite
blooms into an eternal flower, with the
lightness and delicate finish as well as the
aerial proportion and perspective of vege-

table beauty." Then when he has re-
covered from the shock of this, here is my
second : " Nor can any lover of nature
enter the old piles of Oxford and English
cathedrals without feeling that the forest
overpowered the mind of the builder, and
that his chisel, his saw and plane, still re-
produced its ferns, its spikes of flowers,
its locust, elm, pine, and spruce."

Memoranda : *Lincoln choir is an example
of Early English or First Pointed, which
can generally be told from something else by
bold projecting buttresses and dog-tooth mould-
ing round the abacusses.* (The plural is my
own, and it does not look right.) *Lincoln
Castle was the scene of many prolonged sieges,
and was once taken by Oliver Cromwell.*

·   ·   ·   ·   ·   ·   ·   ·

HE

YORK, *June* 24.
The Black Swan.

Kitty Schuyler is the concentrated essence of feminine witchery. Intuition
strong, logic weak, and the two qualities
so balanced as to produce an indefinable

charm ; will-power large, but docility equal,
if a man is clever enough to know how to
manage her ; knowledge of facts absolutely
nil, but she is exquisitely intelligent in
spite of it. She has a way of evading,
escaping, eluding, and then gives you an
intoxicating hint of sudden and complete
surrender. She is divinely innocent, but
roguishness saves her from insipidity.
Her looks? She looks as you would imagine a person might look who possessed
these graces; and she is worth looking at,
though every time I do it I have a rush
of love to the head. When you find a
girl who combines all the qualities you
have imagined in the ideal, and who has
added a dozen or two on her own account,
merely to distract you past all hope, why
stand up and try to resist her charm?
Down on your knees like a man, say I !

.   .   .   .

I 'm getting to adore aunt Celia. I
did n't care for her at first, but she is so
deliciously blind! Anything more exquisitely unserviceable as a chaperon I
can't imagine. Absorbed in antiquity, she
ignores the babble of contemporaneous

lovers. That any man could look at
Kitty when he could look at a cathedral
passes her comprehension. I do not presume too greatly on her absent-minded-
ness, however, lest she should turn unex-
pectedly and rend me. I always remember
that inscription on the backs of the little
mechanical French toys, — " Quoiqu'elle
soit très solidement montée, il faut ne pas
brutaliser la machine."

And so my courtship progresses under
aunt Celia's very nose. I say " progresses," but it is impossible to speak
with any certainty of courting, for the essence of that gentle craft is hope, rooted
in labor and trained by love.

I set out to propose to her during service this afternoon by writing my feelings
on the fly-leaf of the hymn-book, or something like that ; but I knew that aunt Celia
would never forgive such blasphemy, and
I thought that Kitty herself might consider
it wicked. Besides, if she should chance
to accept me, there was nothing I could
do, in a cathedral, to relieve my feelings.
No ; if she ever accepts me, I wish it to
be in a large, vacant spot of the universe,

peopled by two only, and those two so indistinguishably blended, as it were, that they would appear as one to the casual observer. So I practiced repression, though the wall of my reserve is worn to the thinness of thread-paper, and I tried to keep my mind on the droning minor canon, and not to look at her, "for that way madness lies."

.   .   .   .

SHE

York, *June* 26.
High Petersgate Street.

My taste is so bad! I just begin to realize it, and I am feeling my "growing pains," like · Gwendolen in "Daniel Deronda." I admired the stained glass in the Lincoln Cathedral, especially the Nuremberg window. I thought Mr. Copley looked pained, but he said nothing. When I went to my room, I looked in a book and found that all the glass in that cathedral is very modern and very bad, and the Nuremberg window is the worst of all. Aunt Celia says she hopes that it will be a warning to me to read before I speak ; but Mr. Copley says no, that the world would lose more in one way than it would gain in the other. I tried my quotations this morning, and stuck fast in the middle of the first.

Mr. Copley says that aunt Celia has been feeing the vergers altogether too much, and I wrote a song about it called "The Ballad of the Vergers and the Foolish Virgin," which I sang to my guitar. Mr. Copley says it is cleverer than anything he ever did with his pencil, but of course he says that only to be agreeable.

We all went to an evening service last night. Coming home, aunt Celia walked ahead with Mrs. Benedict, who keeps turning up at the most unexpected moments. She 's going to build a Gothicky memorial chapel somewhere. I don't know for whom, unless it 's for Benedict Arnold. I don't like her in the least, but four is certainly a more comfortable number than three. I scarcely ever have a moment alone with Mr. Copley ; for go where I will and do what I please, aunt Celia has the most perfect confidence in my indiscretion, so she is always *en évidence*.

Just as we were turning into the quiet little street where we are, lodging I said, " Oh dear, I wish that I knew something about architecture ! "

" If you don't know anything about it, you are certainly responsible for a good deal of it," said Mr. Copley.

" I ? How do you mean ? " I asked quite innocently, because I could n't see how he could twist such a remark as that into anything like sentiment.

" I have never built so many castles in my life as since I 've known you, Miss Schuyler," he said.

"Oh," I answered as lightly as I could, "air-castles don't count."

" The building of air-castles is an innocent amusement enough, I suppose," he said, " but I 'm committing the folly of living in mine. I " —

Then I was frightened. When, all at once, you find you have something precious you only dimly suspected was to be yours, you almost wish it had n't come so soon. But just at that moment Mrs. Benedict called to us, and came tramping back from the gate, and hooked her supercilious, patronizing arm in Mr. Copley's, and asked him into the sitting-room to talk over the "lady chapel" in her new memorial church. Then aunt Celia told me they would excuse me, as I had had a wearisome day; and there was nothing for me to do but to go to bed, like a snubbed child, and wonder if I should ever know the end of that sentence. And I listened at the head of the stairs, shivering, but all that I could hear was that Mrs. Benedict asked Mr. Copley to be her own architect. Her architect indeed! That woman ought not to be at large!

.   .   .   .

DURHAM, *July* 15.
At Farmer Hendry's.

We left York this morning, and arrived here about eleven o'clock. It seems there is some sort of an election going on in the town, and there was not a single fly at the station. Mr. Copley walked about in every direction, but neither horse nor vehicle was to be had for love nor money. At last we started to walk to the village, Mr. Copley so laden with our hand-luggage

that he resembled a pack-mule. We made
a tour of the inns, but not a single room
was to be had, not for that night nor for
three days ahead, on account of that same
election.

" Had n't we better go on to Edinburgh,
aunt Celia ? " I asked.

" Edinburgh? Never ! " she replied.
" Do you suppose that I would voluntarily
spend a Sunday in those bare Presbyterian
churches until the memory of these past
ideal weeks has faded a little from my
memory? What, leave out Durham and
spoil the set ? " (She spoke of the cathedrals as if they were souvenir spoons.)
" I intended to stay here for a week or
more, and write up a record of our entire
trip from Winchester while the impressions
were fresh in my mind."

" And I had intended doing the same
thing." said Mr. Copley. " That is, I
hoped to finish off my previous sketches,
which are in a frightful state of incomple-
tion, and spend a good deal of time on
the interior of this cathedral, which is unusually beautiful." (At this juncture aunt
Celia disappeared for a moment to ask the

barmaid if, in her opinion, the constant consumption of malt liquors prevents a more dangerous indulgence in brandy and whiskey. She is gathering statistics, but as the barmaids can never collect their thoughts while they are drawing ale, aunt Celia proceeds slowly.)

" For my part," said I, with mock humility, " I am a docile person who never has any intentions of her own, but who yields herself sweetly to the intentions of other people in her immediate vicinity."

" Are you ? " asked Mr. Copley, taking out his pencil.

" Yes, I said so. What are you doing ? "

" Merely taking note of your statement, that's all. — Now, Miss Van Tyck, I have a plan to propose. I was here last summer with a couple of Harvard men, and we lodged at a farmhouse half a mile from the cathedral. If you will step into the coffee-room of the Shoulder of Mutton and Cauliflower for an hour, I'll walk up to Farmer Hendry's and see if they will take us in. I think we might be fairly comfortable."

"Can aunt Celia have Apollinaris and black coffee after her morning bath?" I asked.

"I hope, Katharine," said aunt Celia majestically, — "I hope that I can accommodate myself to circumstances. If Mr. Copley can secure lodgings for us, I shall be more than grateful."

So here we are, all lodging together in an ideal English farmhouse. There is a thatched roof on one of the old buildings, and the dairy house is covered with ivy, and Farmer Hendry's wife makes a real English courtesy, and there are herds of beautiful sleek Durham cattle, and the butter and cream and eggs and mutton are delicious; and I never, never want to go home any more. I want to live here forever, and wave the American flag on Washington's birthday.

I am so happy that I feel as if something were going to spoil it all. Twenty years old to-day! I wish mamma were alive to wish me many happy returns.

Memoranda: Casual remark for breakfast table or perhaps for luncheon. — it is a trifle heavy for breakfast: "*Since the sixteenth century and despite the work of Inigo Jones and the great Wren* (not Jenny Wren — Christopher), *architecture has had, in England especially, no legitimate development."*

.   .   .   .   .   .   -   .

HE

DURHAM, *July* 19.

O child of fortune, thy name is J. Q. Copley! How did it happen to be election time? Why did the inns chance to be full? How did aunt Celia relax sufficiently to allow me to find her a lodging? Why did she fall in love with the lodging when found? I do not know. I only know Fate smiles; that Kitty and I eat our morning bacon and eggs together; that I carve Kitty's cold beef and pour Kitty's sparkling ale at luncheon; that I go to vespers with Kitty, and dine with Kitty, and walk in the gloaming with Kitty — and aunt Celia. And after a day of heaven like this, like Lorna Doone's lover, — ay, and like every other lover, I suppose, — I go to sleep, and the roof above

me swarms with angels, having Kitty
under it !

We were coming home from afternoon
service, Kitty and I. (I am anticipating,
for she was "Miss Schuyler" then, but
never mind.) We were walking through
the fields, while Mrs. Benedict and aunt
Celia were driving. As we came across a
corner of the bit of meadow land that
joins the stable and the garden, we heard
a muffled roar, and as we looked round
we saw a creature with tossing horns and
waving tail making for us, head down,
eyes flashing. Kitty gave a shriek. We
chanced to be near a pair of low bars. I
had n't been a college athlete for nothing.
I swung Kitty over the bars, and jumped
after her. But she, not knowing in her
fright where she was nor what she was
doing; supposing, also, that the mad creature, like the villain in the play, would "still
pursue her," flung herself bodily into my
arms, crying, "Jack! Jack! Save me!"

It was the first time she had called me
"Jack," and I needed no second invita-
tion. I proceeded to save her, — in the
usual way, by holding her to my heart and

kissing her lovely hair reassuringly, as I murmured : "You are safe, my darling; not a hair of your precious head shall be hurt. Don't be frightened."

She shivered like a leaf. " I am frightened," she said. " I can't help being frightened. He will chase us, I know. Where is he? What is he doing now ? "

Looking up to determine if I need abbreviate this blissful moment, I saw the enraged animal disappearing in the side door of the barn; and it was a nice, comfortable Durham cow, — that somewhat rare but possible thing, a sportive cow !

" Is he gone ? " breathed Kitty from my waistcoat.

"Yes, he is gone — she is gone, darling. But don't move; it may come again."

My first too hasty assurance had calmed Kitty's fears, and she raised her charming flushed face from its retreat and prepared to withdraw. I did not facilitate the preparations, and a moment of awkward silence ensued.

"Might I inquire," I asked, "if the dear little person at present reposing in my arms will stay there (with intervals for rest and refreshment) for the rest of her natural life ? "

She withdrew entirely now, all but her hand, and her eyes sought the ground.

" I suppose I shall have to now, — that is, if you think — at least, I suppose you do think — at any rate, you look as if you were thinking — that this has been giving you encouragement."

" I do indeed, — decisive, undoubted, barefaced encouragement."

" I don't think I ought to be judged as if I were in my sober senses," she replied. " I was frightened within an inch of my life. I told you this morning that I was dreadfully afraid of bulls, especially mad ones, and I told you that my nurse frightened me, when I was a child, with awful stories about them, and that I never outgrew my childish terror. I looked everywhere about: the barn was too far, the fence too high, I saw him coming, and there was nothing but you and the open country; of course I took you. It was very natural, I 'm sure, — any girl would have done it."

"To be sure," I replied soothingly, "any girl would have run after me, as you say."

"I did n't say any girl would have run after you, — you need n't flatter yourself; and besides, I think I was really trying to protect you as well as to gain protection; else why should I have cast myself on you like a catamount, or a catacomb, or whatever the thing is?"

"Yes, darling, I thank you for saving my life, and I am willing to devote the remainder of it to your service as a pledge of my gratitude; but if you should take up life-saving as a profession, dear, don't throw yourself on a fellow with " —

"Jack! Jack!" she cried, putting her hand over my lips, and getting it well kissed in consequence. "If you will only forget that, and never, never taunt me with it afterwards, I 'll — I 'll — well, I 'll do anything in reason; yes, even marry you!"

CANTERBURY, *July* 31.
The Royal Fountain.

.   .   .   .

I was never sure enough of Kitty, at
first, to dare risk telling her about that
little mistake of hers.   She is such an
elusive person that I spend all my time
in wooing her, and can never lay flatter-
ing unction to my soul that she is really
won.

But after aunt Celia had looked up my
family record and given a provisional con-
sent, and papa Schuyler had cabled a
reluctant blessing, I did not feel capable
of any further self-restraint.

It was twilight here in Canterbury, and
we were sitting on the vine-shaded ve-
randa of aunt Celia's lodging.   Kitty's
head was on my shoulder.   There is something very queer about that ; when Kitty's
head is on my shoulder, I am not capable
of any consecutive train of thought.   When
she puts it there I see stars, then myriads
of stars, then, oh ! I can't begin to enu-
merate the steps by which ecstasy mounts
to delirium ; but at all events, any opera-

tion which demands exclusive use of the intellect is beyond me at these times. Still I gathered my stray wits together and said, " Kitty ! "

" Yes, Jack ? "

" Now that nothing but death or marriage can separate us, I have something to confess to you."

" Yes," she said serenely, " I know what you are going to say.   He was a cow."

I lifted her head from my shoulder sternly, and gazed into her childlike, candid eyes.

" You mountain of deceit !   How long have you known about it ? "

" Ever since the first.   Oh, Jack, stop looking at me in that way !   Not the very first, not when I — not when you — not when we — no, not then, but the next morning, I said to Farmer Hendry, ' I wish you would keep your savage bull chained up while we are here ; aunt Celia is awfully afraid of them, especially those that go mad, like yours ! '   ' Lor', miss,' said Farmer Hendry, ' he have n't been pastured here for three weeks.   I keep him six mile away.   There be n't nothing but

gentle cows in the home medder.' But I
did n't think that you knew, you secre-
tive person! I dare say you planned the
whole thing in advance, in order to take
advantage of my fright!"

"Never! I am incapable of such an
unnecessary subterfuge! Besides, Kitty,
I could not have made an accomplice of a
cow, you know."

"Then," she said, with great dignity,
"if you had been a gentleman and a man
of honor, you would have cried, 'Unhand
me, girl! You are clinging to me under
a misunderstanding!'"

SHE

CHESTER, *August* 8.
The Grosvenor.

Jack and I are going over this same
ground next summer, on our wedding trip.
We shall sail for home next week, and we
have n't half done justice to the cathedrals. After the first two, we saw nothing
but each other on a general background
of architecture. I hope my mind is improved, but oh, I am so hazy about all

the facts I have read since I knew Jack!
Winchester and Salisbury stand out su-
perbly in my memory. They acquired their
ground before it was occupied with other
matters. I shall never forget, for instance,
that Winchester has the longest spire and
Salisbury the highest nave of all the English cathedrals. And I shall never forget
so long as I live that Jane Austen and
Isaac Newt— Oh dear! was it Isaac
Newton or Izaak Walton that was buried
in Winchester and Salisbury? To think
that that interesting fact should have
slipped from my mind, after all the trouble I took with it! But I know that it
was Isaac somebody, and that he was
buried in — well, he was buried in one of
those two places. I am not certain which,
but I can ask Jack; he is sure to know.

PENELOPE'S ENGLISH EXPE-RIENCES

PART FIRST : IN TOWN

I

SMITH'S HOTEL.
10 Dovermarle Street.

HERE we are in London again, — Francesca, Salemina, and I. Salemina is a philanthropist of the Boston philanthropists, limited. I am an artist. Francesca is — It is very difficult to label Francesca. She is, at her present stage of development, just a nice girl; that is about all: the sense of humanity has n't dawned upon her yet; she is even unaware that personal responsibility for the universe has come into vogue, and so she is happy.

Francesca is short of twenty years old, Salemina short of forty, I short of thirty.

Francesca is in love, Salemina never has been in love, I never shall be in love. Francesca is rich, Salemina is well-to-do, I am poor. There we are in a nutshell.

We are not only in London again, but we are again in Smith's private hotel; one of those deliciously comfortable and ensnaring hostelries in Mayfair which one enters as a solvent human being, and which one leaves as a bankrupt, no matter what may be the number of ciphers on one's letter of credit; since the greater one's apparent supply of wealth, the greater the demand made upon it. I never stop long in London without determining to give up my art for a private hotel. There must be millions in it, but I fear I lack some of the essential qualifications for success. I never could have the heart, for example, to charge a struggling young genius eight shillings a week for two candles, and then eight shillings the next week for the same two candles, which the struggling young genius, by dint of vigorous economy, has managed to preserve to a decent height. No, I could never do it, not even if I were certain that she would squander the sixteen shillings in Bond Street fripperies instead of laying them up against the rainy day.

II

It is Salemina who always unsnarls the weekly bill. Francesca spends an evening or two with it, first of all, because, since she is so young, we think it good mental training for her. Not that she ever accomplishes any results worth mentioning. She begins by making three columns, headed respectively F., S., and P.

These initials stand for Francesca, Salemina, and Penelope, but they resemble the signs for pounds, shillings, and pence so perilously that they introduce an added distraction.

She then places in each column the items in which we are all equal, such as rooms, attendance, and lights. Then come the extras, which are different for each person : more ale for one, more hot baths for another ; more carriages for one, more lemon squashes for another. Francesca's column is principally filled with carriages

and lemon squashes. You would fancy
her whole time was spent in driving and
drinking, if you judged her merely by this
weekly statement at the hotel. When she
has reached the point of dividing the
whole bill into three parts, so that each person may know what is her share, she adds
the three together, expecting, not unnat-
urally, to get the total amount of the bill.
Not at all. She never comes within thirty
shillings of the desired amount, and she
is often three or four guineas to the good
or to the bad. One of her difficulties lies
in her inability to remember that in English money it makes a difference where
you place a figure, whether in the pound,
shilling, or pence column. Having been
educated on the theory that a six is a six
the world over, she charged me with sixty
shillings' worth of Apollinaris in one week.
I pounced on the error, and found that
she had jotted down each pint in the shilling instead of in the pence column.

After Francesca has broken ground on
the bill in this way, Salemina, on the next
leisure evening, draws a large armchair
under the lamp and puts on her eyeglasses.

We perch on either arm, and, after iden-
tifying our own extras, we leave her toil-
ing like Cicero in his retirement at Tus-
culum. By midnight she has generally
brought the account to a point where
a half-hour's fresh attention in the early
morning will finish it. Not that she makes
it come out right to a penny. She has
been treasurer of the Boston Band of
Benevolence, of the Saturday Morning
Slöjd Circle, of the Club for the Recep-
tion of Russian Refugees, and of the
Society for the Brooding of Buddhism;
but none of these organizations carries
on its existence by means of pounds, shillings, and pence, or Salemina's resigna-
tion would have been requested long ago.
However, we are not disposed to be cap-
tious; we are too glad to get rid of the bill.
If our united thirds make four or five shillings in excess, we divide them equally;
if it comes the other way about, we make
it up in the same manner; always meeting the sneers of masculine critics with
Dr. Holmes's remark that a faculty for
numbers is a sort of detached-lever ar-
rangement that can be put into a mighty
poor watch.

III

Salemina is so English! I can't think how she manages. She had not been an hour on British soil before she asked a servant to fetch in some coals and mend the fire; she followed this Anglicism by a request for a grilled chop, "a grilled, chump chop, waiter, please," and so on from triumph to triumph. She now discourses of methylated spirits as if she had never in her life heard of alcohol, and all the English equivalents for Americanisms are ready for use on the tip of her tongue. She says "conserv't'ry" and "observ't'ry;" she calls the chambermaid "Mairy," which is infinitely softer, to be sure, than the American "Mary," with its over-long $\bar{a}$; she ejaculates, "Quite so!" in all the pauses of conversation, and talks of smoke-rooms, and camisoles, and luggage-vans, and slip-bodies, and trams, and mangling, and goffering. She also eats jam for breakfast as if she had been reared on it, when every one knows that the average American has to contract the jam habit by patient and continuous practice.

This instantaneous assimilation of English customs does not seem to be affectation on Salemina's part; nor will I wrong her by fancying that she went through a course of training before she left Boston. From the moment she landed you could see that her foot was on her native heath. She inhaled the fog with a sense of intoxication that the east winds of New England had never given her, and a great throb of patriotism swelled in her breast when she first met the Princess of Wales in Hyde Park.

As for me, I get on charmingly with the English nobility and sufficiently well with the gentry, but the upper servants strike terror to my soul. There is something awe-inspiring to me about an English butler. If they would only put him in livery, or make him wear a silver badge; anything, in short, to temper his pride and prevent one from mistaking him for the master of the house or the bishop within his gates. When I call upon Lady DeWolfe, I say to myself impressively, as I go up the steps: " You are as good as a butler, as well born and well bred as a butler, even more intel-

ligent than a butler. Now, simply because
he has an unapproachable haughtiness of
demeanor, which you can respectfully ad-
mire, but can never hope to imitate, do
not cower beneath the polar light of his
eye ; assert yourself ; be a woman ; be an
American citizen ! " All in vain. The
moment the door opens I ask for Lady
DeWolfe in so timid a tone that I know
Parker thinks me the parlor maid's sister
who has rung the visitor's bell by mistake.
If my lady is within, I follow Parker to
the drawing-room, my knees shaking under me at the prospect of committing some
solecism in his sight. Lady DeWolfe's
husband has been noble only four months,
and Parker of course knows it, and perhaps affects even greater *hauteur* to divert
the attention of the vulgar commoner from
the newness of the title.

Dawson, our butler at Smith's private
hotel, wields the same blighting influence
on our spirits, accustomed to the soft
solicitations of the negro waiter or the
comfortable indifference of the free-born
American. We never indulge in ordinary
democratic or frivolous conversation when

"Unapproachable haughtiness of demeanor"

Dawson is serving us at dinner. We "talk up" to him so far as we are able, and before we utter any remark we inquire mentally whether he is likely to think it good form. Accordingly, I maintain throughout dinner a lofty height of aristocratic elegance that impresses even the impassive Dawson, towards whom it is solely directed. To the amazement and amusement of Salemina (who always takes my cheerful inanities at their face value), I give an hypothetical account of my afternoon engagements, interlarding it so thickly with countesses and marchionesses and lords and honorables that though Dawson has passed soup to duchesses, and scarcely ever handed a plate to anything less than a baroness, he dilutes the customary scorn of his glance, and makes it two parts condescending approval as it rests on me, Penelope Hamilton, of the great American working class (unlimited).

IV

Apropos of the servants, it seems to me that the British footman has relaxed a trifle since we were last here ; or is it possible that he reaches the height of his immobility at the height of the London season, and as it declines does he decline and become flesh ?   At all events, I have twice seen a footman change his weight from one leg to the other, as he stood at a shop entrance with his lady's mantle over his arm ; twice have I seen one scratch his chin, and several times have I observed others, during this month of August, conduct themselves in many respects like animate objects with vital organs.   Lest this incendiary statement be challenged, leveled as it is at an institution whose stability and order are but feebly represented by the eternal march of the stars in their courses, I hasten to explain that in none of these cases cited was it a powdered footman who (to use a Delsartean expression) withdrew will from his body and devitalized it before the public eye.   I have observed that the powdered personage has much greater control over his muscles than the ordinary footman with human hair, and is infinitely his superior in rigidity.

I tremble to think of what the powdered

footman may become when he unbends in
the bosom of his family. When, in the
privacy of his own apartments, the powder
is washed off, the canary-seed pads removed from his aristocratic calves, and his
scarlet and buff magnificence exchanged
for a simple *négligé*, I should think he
might be guilty of almost any indiscretion
or violence. I for one would never con-
sent to be the wife and children of a
powdered footman, and receive him in his
moments of reaction.

V

Is it to my credit, or to my eternal
dishonor, that I once made a powdered
footman smile, and that, too, when he was
handing a buttered muffin to an earl's
daughter?

It was while we were paying a visit at
Marjorimallow Hall, Sir Owen and Lady
Marjorimallow's place in Surrey. This
was to be our first appearance in an English country house, and we made elaborate
preparations. Only our freshest toilets
were packed, and these were arranged in

our trunks with the sole view of impressing
the lady's maid who should unpack them.
We each purchased dressing-cases and
new toilet articles, Francesca's being of
sterling silver, Salemina's of triple plate,
and mine of celluloid, as befitted our
several fortunes. Salemina read up on
English politics; Francesca practiced a
new way of dressing her hair; and I made
up a portfolio of sketches. We counted,
therefore, on representing American letters, beauty, and art to that portion of the
great English public staying at Marjorimallow Hall. (I must interject a paren-
thesis here to the effect that matters did
not move precisely as we expected; for at
table, where most of our time was passed,
Francesca had for a neighbor a scientist,
who asked her plump whether the religion
of the American Indian was or was not a
pure theism; Salemina's partner objected
to the word " politics " in the mouth of a
woman; while my attendant squire adored
a good bright-colored chromo. But this
is anticipating.)

Three days before our departure, I remarked at the breakfast table, Dawson

being absent : " My dear girls, you are aware that we have ordered fried eggs, scrambled eggs, and poached eggs ever since we came to Dovermarle Street, simply because we cannot eat boiled eggs prettily from the shell, English fashion, and cannot break them into a cup or a glass, American fashion, on account of the effect upon Dawson. Now there will certainly be boiled eggs at Marjorimallow Hall, and we cannot refuse them morning after morning ; it will be cowardly (which is unpleasant), and it will be remarked (which is worse). Eating them from an egg-cup, in a baronial hall, with the remains of a drawbridge in the grounds, is equally impossible ; if we do that, Lady Marjorimallow will be having our luggage examined, to see if we carry wigwams and war whoops about with us. No, it is clearly necessary that we master the gentle art of eating eggs tidily and daintily from the shell. I have seen Englishwomen — very dull ones, too — do it without apparent effort ; I have even seen an English infant do it, and that without soiling her apron, or, as Salemina would say, ' messing her pinafore.' I propose, therefore, that we order soft-boiled eggs daily ; that we send Dawson from the room directly breakfast is served ; and that then and there we have a class for opening eggs, lowest grade, object method. Any person who cuts the shell badly, or permits the egg to leak over the rim, or allows yellow dabs on the plate, or upsets the cup, or stains her fingers, shall be fined 'tuppence' and locked into her bedroom for five minutes."

The first morning we were all in the bedroom together, and, there being no innocent person to collect fines, the wildest civil disorder prevailed.

On the second day Salemina and I improved slightly, but Francesca had passed a sleepless night, and her hand trembled (the love-letter mail had come in from America). We were obliged to tell her, as we collected " tuppence " twice on the same egg, that she must either remain at home, or take an oilcloth apron to Marjorimallow Hall.

But "ease is the lovely result of forgotten toil," and it is only a question of

time and desire with Americans; we are
so clever. Other nations have to be
trained from birth; but as we need only an
ounce of training where they need a pound,
we can afford to procrastinate. Sometimes we procrastinate too long, but that
is a trifle. On the third morning success
crowned our efforts. Salemina smiled,
and I told an anecdote, during the opera-
tion, although my egg was cracked in the
boiling, and I question if the Queen's
favorite maid of honor could have managed it prettily. Accordingly, when eggs
were brought to the breakfast table at
Marjorimallow Hall, we were only slightly
nervous. Francesca was at the far end of
the long table, and I do not know how
she fared, but from various Anglicisms
that Salemina dropped, as she chatted
with the Queen's Counsel on her left, I
could see that her nerve was steady and
circulation free. We exchanged glances
(there was the mistake!), and with an
excited laugh she struck her egg a hasty
blow.

Her egg-cup slipped and lurched; a top
fraction of the egg flew in the direction

of the Q. C., and the remaining portion
oozed, in yellow confusion, rapidly into
her plate. Alas for that past mistress of
elegant dignity, Salemina! If I had been at
her Majesty's table, I should have smiled,
even if I had gone to the Tower the next
moment ; but as it was, I became hysteri-
cal. My neighbor, a portly member of
Parliament, looked amazed, Salemina grew
scarlet, the situation was charged with
danger ; and, rapidly viewing the various
exits, I chose the humorous one, and told
as picturesquely as possible the whole
story of our school of egg-opening in
Dovermarle Street, the highly arduous and
encouraging rehearsals conducted there,
and the stupendous failure incident to our
first public appearance. Sir Owen led
the good-natured laughter and applause ;
lords and ladies, Q. C.'s and M. P.'s,
joined in with a will; poor Salemina
raised her drooping head, opened and ate
a second egg with the repose of a Vere de
Vere — and the footman smiled!

VI

I do not see why we hear that the Eng-lishman is deficient in a sense of humor. His jokes may not be a matter of daily food to him, as they are to the American ; he may not love whimsicality with the same passion, nor inhale the aroma of a witticism with as keen a relish ; but he likes fun whenever he sees it, and he sees it as often as most people. It may be that we find the Englishman more re-ceptive to our bits of feminine nonsense just now, simply because this is the day of the American woman in London, and, having been assured that she is an enter-taining personage, young John Bull is will-ing to take it for granted so long as she does n't want to marry him, and even this pleasure he will allow her on occasion, — if well paid for it.

The longer I live, the more I feel it an absurdity to label nations with national traits, and then endeavor to make individ-uals conform to the required standard. It is possible, I suppose, to draw certain broad distinctions, though even these are subject to change ; but the habit of generalizing from one particular, that mainstay of the cheap and obvious essayist, has rooted many fictions in the public mind. Nothing, for instance, can blot from my memory the profound, searching, and exhaustive analysis of a great nation which I learned in my small geography when I was a child, namely, " The French are a gay and polite people, fond of dancing and light wines."

One young Englishman whom I have met lately errs on the side of over-appreciation. He laughs before, during, and after every remark I make, unless it be a simple request for food or drink. This is an acquaintance of Willie Beresford, the Honorable Arthur Ponsonby, who was the " whip " on our coach drive to Dorking, — dear, delightful, adorable Dorking, of hen celebrity.

Salemina insisted on my taking the box seat, in the hope that the Honorable Arthur would amuse me. She little knew him ! He sapped me of all my ideas, and gave me none in exchange. Anything so unspeakably heavy I never encountered.

It is very difficult for a woman who does
n't know a nigh horse from an off one,
nor the wheelers from the headers (or is it
the fronters?), to find subjects of conversation with a gentleman who spends three
fourths of his existence on a coach. It
was the more difficult for me because I
could not decide whether Willie Beresford
was cross because I was devoting myself
to the whip, or because Francesca had remained at home with a headache. This
state of affairs continued for about fifteen
miles, when it suddenly dawned upon the
Honorable Arthur that, however mistaken
my speech and manner, I was trying to
be agreeable. This conception acted on
the honest and amiable soul like magic.
I gradually became comprehensible, and
finally he gave himself up to the theory
that, though eccentric, I was harmless and
amusing, so we got on famously, — so
famously that Willie Beresford grew ri-
diculously gloomy, and I decided that it
could not be Francesca's headache.

The names of these English streets are
a never-failing source of delight to me.
In that one morning we drove past Pie,

Pudding, and Petticoat Lanes, and later on we found ourselves in a " Prudent Passage," which opened, very inappropriately, into " Huggin Lane." Willie Beresford said it was the first time he had ever heard of anything so disagreeable as prudence terminating in anything so agreeable as huggin'. When he had been severely reprimanded by Mrs. Beresford for this shocking speech, I said to the Honorable Arthur : —

" I don't understand your business signs in England, — this ' Company, Limited,' and that ' Company, Limited.' That one, of course, is quite plain " (pointing to the front of a building on the village street), " ' Goat's Milk Company, Limited ; ' I suppose they have but one or two goats, and necessarily the milk must be limited."

Salemina says that this was not in the least funny, that it was absolutely flat ; but it had quite the opposite effect upon the Honorable Arthur. He had no command over himself or his horses for some. minutes ; and at intervals during the afternoon the full felicity of the idea would steal upon him, and the smile of reminiscence would flit across his ruddy face.

The next day, at the Eton and Harrow games at Lord's cricket ground, he presented three flowers of British aristocracy to our party, and asked me each time to tell the goat story, which he had previously told himself, and probably murdered in the telling. Not content with this arrant flattery, he begged to be allowed to recount some of my international episodes to a literary friend who writes for Punch. I demurred decidedly, but Salemina said that perhaps I ought to be willing to lower myself a trifle for the sake of elevating Punch ! This home thrust so delighted the Honorable Arthur that it remained his favorite joke for days, and the overworked goat was permitted to enjoy that oblivion from which Salemina insists it should never have emerged.

VII

The Honorable Arthur, Salemina, and I took a stroll in Hyde Park one Sunday afternoon, not for the purpose of joining the fashionable throng of " pretty people " at Stanhope Gate, but to mingle with the common herd in its special precincts, — precincts not set apart, indeed, by any legal formula, but by a natural law of classification which seems to be inherent in the universe. It was a curious and motley crowd, a little dull, perhaps, but orderly, well behaved, and self-respecting, with here and there part of the flotsam and jetsam of a great city, a ragged, sodden, hopeless wretch wending his way about with the rest, thankful for any diversion.

Under the trees, each in the centre of his group, large or small according to his magnetism and eloquence, stood the park "shouter," airing his special grievance, playing his special part, preaching his special creed, pleading his special cause, — anything, probably, for the sake of shouting. We were plainly dressed, and did not attract observation as we joined the outside circle of one of these groups after another. It was as interesting to watch the listeners as the speakers. I wished I might paint the sea of faces, eager, anxious, stolid, attentive, happy, and unhappy : histories written on many of them ; others blank, unmarked by any thought or aspiration. I stole a sidelong look at the Honorable Arthur. He is an Englishman first, and a man afterwards (I prefer it the other way), but he does not realize it; he thinks he is just like all other good fellows, but he is mistaken. He and Willie Beresford speak the same language, but they are as different as Malay and Eskimo. He is an extreme type, but he is very likable and very well worth looking at, with his long coat, his silk hat, and the white Malmaison in his buttonhole. He is always so radiantly, fascinatingly clean, the Honorable Arthur, simple, frank, direct, sensible, and he bores me almost to tears.

The first orator was edifying his hearers with an explanation of the drama of " The Corsican Brothers," and his eloquence, unlike that of the other speakers, was largely inspired by the hope of pennies. It was a novel idea, and his interpretation was rendered very amusing to us by the wholly original Yorkshire accent which he gave to the French personages and places in the play.

An Irishman in black clerical garb held

the next group together. He was in some
trouble, owing to a pig-headed and quar-
relsome Scotchman in the front rank, who
objected to each statement that fell from
his lips, thus interfering seriously with the
effect of his peroration. If the Irishman
had been more convincing, I suppose the
crowd would have silenced the scoffer, for
these little matters of discipline are always
attended to by the audience; but the
Scotchman's points were too well taken ;
he was so trenchant, in fact, at times, that
a voice would cry, " Coom up, Sandy, an
'ave it all yer own w'y, boy ! " The discussion continued as long as we were
within hearing distance, for the Irishman,
though amiable and ignorant, was firm, the
" unconquered Scot " was on his native
heath of argument, and the little knot of
listeners were willing to give them both a
hearing.

Under the next tree a fluent cockney
lad of sixteen or eighteen years was de-
claiming his bitter experiences with the
Salvation Army. He had been sheltered
in one of its beds which was not to his
taste, and it had found employment for

him which he had to walk twenty-two miles to get, and which was not to his liking when he did get it. A meeting of the Salvation Army at a little distance rendered his speech more interesting, as its points were repeated and denied as fast as made.

Of course there were religious groups and temperance groups, and groups devoted to the tearing down or raising up of most things except the government; for on that day there were no Anarchist and Socialist shouters, as is ordinarily the case.

As we strolled down one of the broad roads under the shade of the noble trees, we saw the sun setting in a red-gold haze; a glory of vivid color made indescribably tender and opalescent by the kind of luminous mist that veils it; a wholly English sunset, and an altogether lovely one. And quite away from the other knots of people, there leaned against a bit of wire fence a poor old man surrounded by half a dozen children and one tired woman with a nursing baby. He had a tattered book, which seemed to be the story of the

Gospels, and his little flock sat on the greensward at his feet as he read. It may be that he, too, had been a shouter in his lustier manhood, and had held a larger audience together by the power of his belief; but now he was helpless to attract any but the children. Whether it was the pathos of his white hairs, his garb of shreds and patches, or the mild benignity of his eye that moved me, I know not, but among all the Sunday shouters in Hyde Park it seemed to me that that quavering voice of the past spoke with the truest note.

VIII

The English Park Lover, loving his love on a green bench in Kensington Gardens or Regent's Park, or indeed in any spot where there is a green bench, so long as it is within full view of the passer-by, — this English public Lover, male or female, is a most interesting study, for we have not his exact counterpart in America. He is thoroughly respectable, I should think, my urban Colin. He does not have the air of a gay deceiver roving from flower

" Helpless to attract any but the children "

to flower, stealing honey as he goes; he looks, on the contrary, as if it were his intention to lead Phœbe to the altar on the next bank holiday; there is a dead calm in his actions which bespeaks no other course. If Colin were a Don Juan, surely he would be a trifle more ardent, for there is no tropical fervor in his matter-of-fact caresses. He does not embrace Phœbe in the park, apparently, because he adores her to madness; because her smile is like fire in his veins, melting down all his defenses; because the intoxication of her nearness is irresistible; because, in fine, he cannot wait until he finds a more secluded spot: nay, verily, he embraces her because — tell me, infatuated fruiterers, poulterers, soldiers, haberdashers (limited), what is your reason? for it does not appear to the casual eye. Stormy weather does not vex the calm of the Park Lover, for "the rains of Marly do not wet" when one is in love. By a clever manipulation of four arms and four hands they can manage an umbrella and enfold each other at the same time, though a feminine mackintosh is well known to be

ill adapted to the purpose, and a continuous drizzle would dampen almost any
other lover in the universe.

The park embrace, as nearly as I can
analyze it, seems to be one part instinct,
one part duty, one part custom, and one
part reflex action. I have purposely
omitted pleasure (which, in the analysis of
the ordinary embrace, reduces all the other
ingredients to an almost invisible fraction), because I fail to find it; but I am
willing to believe that in some rudimen-
tary form it does exist, because man attends
to no purely unpleasant matter with such
praiseworthy assiduity. Anything more
fixedly stolid than the Park Lover when
he passes his arm round his chosen one
and takes her crimson hand in his, I have
never seen; unless, indeed, it be the fixed
stolidity of the chosen one herself. I had
not at first the assurance even to glance
at them as I passed by, blushing myself
to the roots of my hair, though the of-
fenders themselves never changed color.
Many a time have I walked out of my way
or lowered my parasol, for fear of invad-
ing their Sunday Eden; but a spirit of in-

quiry awoke in me at last, and I began to
make psychological investigations, with a
view to finding out at what point embarrassment would appear in the Park Lover.
I experimented (it was a most arduous
and unpleasant task) with upwards of two
hundred couples, and it is interesting to
record that self-consciousness was not
apparent in a single instance. It was not
merely that they failed to resent my stopping in the path directly opposite them, or
my glaring most offensively at them, nor
that they even allowed me to sit upon
their green bench and witness their chaste
salutes, but it was that they did fail to
perceive me at all! There is a kind of
superb finish and completeness about their
indifference to the public gaze which re-
moves it from ordinary immodesty, and
gives it a certain scientific value.

IX

Among all my English experiences, none
occupies so important a place as my forced
meeting with the Duke of Cimicifugas.
(There can be no harm in my telling the

incident, so long as I do not give the right names, which are very well known to fame.) The Duchess of Cimicifugas, who is charming, unaffected, and lovable, so report says, has among her chosen friends an untitled woman whom we will call Mrs. Apis Mellifica. I met her only daughter, Hilda, in America, and we became quite intimate. It seems that Mrs. Apis Mellifica, who has an income of £20,000 a year, often exchanges presents with the duchess, and at this time she had brought with her from the Continent some rare old tapestries with which to adorn a new morning-room at Cimicifugas House. These tapestries were to be hung during the absence of the duchess in Homburg, and were to greet her as a birthday surprise on her return. Hilda Mellifica, who is one of the most talented amateur artists in London, and who has exquisite taste in all matters of decoration, was to go down to the ducal residence to inspect the work, and she obtained permission from Lady Veratrum (the confidential companion of the duchess) to bring me with her. I started on this journey to the country with all possible delight, little surmising the agonies that lay in store for me in the mercifully hidden future.

The tapestries were perfect, and Lady Veratrum was most amiable and affable, though the blue blood of the Belladonnas courses in her veins, and her great-grandfather was the celebrated Earl of Rhus Tox, who rendered such notable service to his sovereign. We roamed through the splendid apartments, inspected the superb picture gallery, where scores of dead-and-gone Cimicifugases (most of them very plain) were glorified by the art of Van Dyck, Sir Joshua, or Gainsborough, and admired the priceless collections of marbles and cameos and bronzes. It was about four o'clock when we were conducted to a magnificent apartment for a brief rest, as we were to return to London at half past six. As Lady Veratrum left us, she remarked casually, "His Grace will join us at tea."

The door closed, and at the same moment I fell upon the brocaded satin state bed and tore off my hat and gloves like one distraught.

"Hilda," I gasped, "you brought me here, and you must rescue me, for I absolutely decline to drink tea with a duke."

"Nonsense, Penelope, don't be absurd," she replied. "I have never happened to see him myself, and I am a trifle nervous, but it cannot be very terrible, I should think."

"Not to you, perhaps, but to me impossible," I said. "I thought he was in Homburg, or I would never have entered this place. It is not that I fear nobility. I could meet her Majesty the Queen at the Court of St. James without the slightest flutter of embarrassment, because I know I could trust her not to presume on my defenselessness to enter into conversation with me. But this duke, whose dukedom very likely dates back to the hour of the Norman Conquest, is a very different person, and is to be met under very different circumstances. He may ask me my politics. Of course I can tell him that I am a Mugwump, but what if he asks me why I am a Mugwump?"

"He will not," Hilda answered. "Englishmen are not wholly devoid of feeling!"

"And how shall I address him?" I went on. "Does one call him 'your Grace,' or 'your Royal Highness'? Oh, for a thousandth part of the unblushing impertinence of that countrywoman of mine who called your future king 'Tummy'! but she was a beauty, and I am not pretty enough to be anything but discreetly well-mannered. Shall you sit in his presence, or stand and grovel alternately? Does one have to courtesy? Very well, then, make any excuses you like for me, Hilda : say I'm eccentric, say I'm deranged, say I'm a Nihilist. I will hide under the scullery table, fling myself in the moat, lock myself in the keep, let the portcullis fall on me, die any appropriate early English death, — anything rather than courtesy in a tailor-made gown ; I can kneel beautifully, Hilda, if that will do : you remember my ancestors were brought up on kneeling, and yours on courtesying, and it makes a great difference in the muscles."

Hilda smiled benignantly as she wound the coil of russet hair round her shapely head. "He will think whatever you do

charming, and whatever you say brilliant,"
she said ; " that is the advantage in being
an American woman."

X

Just at this moment Lady Veratrum
sent a haughty maid to ask us if we would
meet her under the trees in the park which
surrounds the house. I hailed this as a
welcome reprieve to the dreaded function
of tea with the duke, and made up my
mind, while descending the marble stair-
case, that I would slip away and lose myself accidentally in the grounds, appearing
only in time for the London train. This
happy mode of issue from my difficulties
lent a springiness to my step, as we followed a waxwork footman over the velvet
sward to a nook under a group of copper
beeches. But there, to my dismay, stood
a charmingly appointed tea-table glittering
with silver and Royal Worcester, with several liveried servants bringing cakes and
muffins and berries to Lady Veratrum, who
sat behind the steaming urn. I started
to retreat, when there appeared, walking

towards us, a simple man, with nothing in the least extraordinary about him.

"That cannot be the Duke of Cimicifugas," thought I, "a man in a corduroy jacket, without a sign of a suite ; probably it is a Banished Duke come from the Forest of Arden for a buttered muffin."

But it was the Duke of Cimicifugas, and no other. Hilda was presented first, while I tried to fire my courage by thinking of the Puritan Fathers, and Plymouth Rock, and the Boston Tea-Party, and the battle of Bunker Hill. Then my turn came. I murmured some words which might have been anything, and courtesied in a stiff-necked self-respecting sort of way. Then we talked, — at least the duke and Lady Veratrum talked. Hilda said a few blameless words, such as befitted an untitled English virgin in the presence of the nobility ; while I maintained the probationary silence required by Pythagoras of his first year's pupils. My idea was to observe this first duke without uttering a word, to talk with the second (if I should ever meet a second), to chat with the third, and to secure the fourth for Francesca to take home to America with her.

Of course I know that dukes are very dear, but she could afford any reasonable sum, if she found one whom she fancied; the principal obstacle in the path is that tiresome American lawyer with whom she considers herself in love. I have never gone beyond that first experience, however, for dukes in England are as rare as snakes in Ireland. I can't think why they allow them to die out so, — the dukes, not the snakes. If a country is to have an aristocracy, let there be enough of it, say I, and make it imposing at the top, where it shows most, especially since, as I understand it, all that Victoria has to do is to say, "Let there be dukes," and there are dukes.

XI

Francesca wishes to get some old hall-marked silver for her home tea tray, and she is absorbed at present in answering advertisements of people who have second-hand pieces for sale, and who offer to bring them on approval. The other day, when Willie Beresford and I came in from Westminster Abbey (where we had been

choosing the best locations for our memorial tablets), we thought Francesca must
be giving a " small and early ; " but it
transpired that all the silver-sellers had
called at the same hour, and it took the
united strength of Dawson and Mr. Beresford, together with my diplomacy, to rescue
the poor child from their clutches.   She
came out alive, but her safety was purchased at the cost of a George IV. cream
jug, an Elizabethan sugar bowl, and a
Boadicea tea caddy, which were, I doubt
not, manufactured in Wardour Street towards the close of the nineteenth century.

Salemina came in just then, cold and
tired.   (Tower and National Gallery the
same day.   It's so much more work to
go to the Tower nowadays than it used to
be !)   We had intended to go to Richmond
on a penny steamboat, but it was drizzling,
so we had a cosy fire instead, slipped into
our tea-gowns, and ordered tea and thin
bread and butter, a basket of strawberries
with their frills on, and a jug of Devon-
shire cream.   Willie Beresford asked if
he might stay ;, otherwise, he said, he
should have to sit at a cold marble table

on the corner of Bond Street and Piccadilly, and take his tea in bachelor solitude.

"Yes," I said severely, "we will allow
you to stay; though, as you are coming to
dinner, I should think you would have to
go away some time, if only in order that
you might get ready to come back. You 've
been here since breakfast time."

"Quite so," he answered calmly, "and
my only error in judgment was that I
did n't take an earlier breakfast, in order
to begin my day here sooner. One has
to snatch a moment when he can, nowadays; for these rooms are so infested with
British swells that a base-born American
stands very little chance!"

Now I should like to know if Willie
Beresford is in love with Francesca. What
shall I do — that is, what shall we do —
if he is, when she is in love with somebody
else? To be sure, she may want one
lover for foreign and another for domestic
service. He is too old for her, but that
is always the way. "When Alcides, having gone through all the fatigues of life,
took a bride in Olympus, he ought to have
selected Minerva, but he chose Hebe."

I wonder why so many people call him "Willie" Beresford, at his age. Perhaps it is because his mother sets the example; but from her lips it does not seem amiss. I suppose when she looks at him she recalls the past, and is ever seeing the little child in the strong man, mother fashion. It is very beautiful, that feeling; and when a girl surprises it in any mother's eyes it makes her heart beat faster, as in the presence of something sacred, which she can understand only because she is a woman, and experience is foreshadowed in intuition.

The Honorable Arthur had sent us a dozen London dailies and weeklies, and we fell into an idle discussion of their contents over the teacups. I had found an "exchange column" which was as interesting as it was novel, and I told Francesca it seemed to me that if we managed wisely we could rid ourselves of all our useless belongings, and gradually amass a collection of the English articles we most desired. " Here is an opportunity, for instance," I said, and I read aloud, —

"'S. G., of Kensington, will post "Woman" three days old regularly for a box of cut flowers.'"

"Rather young," said Mr. Beresford, "or I'd answer that advertisement myself."

I wanted to tell him I didn't suppose that he could find anything too young for his taste, but I didn't dare.

"Salemina adores cats," I went on. "How is this, Sally, dear? —

"'A handsome orange male Persian cat, also a tabby, immense coat, brushes and frills, is offered in exchange for an electro-plated revolving covered dish or an Allen's Vapor Bath.'"

"I should like the cat, but alas! I have no covered dish," sighed Salemina.

"Buy one," suggested Mr. Beresford. "Even then you'd be getting a bargain. Do you understand that you receive the male orange cat for the dish, and the frilled tabby for the bath, or do you get both in exchange for either of these articles? Read on, Miss Hamilton."

"Very well, here is one for Francesca:

"'A harmonium with seven stops is

offered in exchange for a really good Plymouth cockerel hatched in May.'"

"I should want to know when the harmonium was hatched," said Francesca prudently. "Now you cannot usurp the platform entirely, my dear Pen. Listen to an English marriage notice from the 'Times.' It chances to be the longest one to-day, but there were others just as remarkable in yesterday's issue.

"'On the 17th instant, at Emmanuel Church (Countess of Padelford's connection), Weston-super-Mare, by the Rev. Canon Vernon, B. D., Rector of St. Edmund the King and Martyr, Suffolk Street, uncle of the bride, assisted by the Rev. Otho Pelham, M. A., Vicar of All Saints, Upper Norwood, Dr. Philosophial Konrad Rasch, of Koetzsenbroda, Saxony, to Evelyn Whitaker Rake, widow of the late Richard Balaclava Rake, Barrister-at-law of the Inner Temple and Bombay, and third surviving daughter of George Frederic Goldspink, C. B., of Craig House, Sydenham Hill, Commissioner of her Majesty's Customs, and formerly of the War Office.'"

By the time this was finished we were
all quite exhausted, but we revived like
magic when Salemina read us her contri-
bution : —

"'A NAME ENSHRINED IN LITERATURE
AND RENOWNED IN COMMERCE, — Miss
Willard, Waddington, Middlesex. Deal
with her whenever you possibly can. When
you want to purchase, ask her for anything
under the canopy of heaven, from jewels,
bijouterie, and curios to rare books and
high-class articles of utility. When you
want to sell, consign only to her, from
choice gems to mundane objects. All
transactions embodying the germs of small
profits are welcome. Don't readily forget
this or her name and address, — Clara
(Miss) Willard (the Lady Trader), Waddington, Middlesex. Immaculate prompti-
tude and scrupulous liberality observed :
therefore, on these credentials, ye must
deal with her ; it is the duty of intellect
to be reciprocal.' "

Just here Dawson entered, evidently to
lay the dinner-cloth, but, seeing that we
had a visitor, he took the tea-tray and
retired discreetly.

" It is five and thirty minutes past six, Mr. Beresford," I said. " Do you think you can get to the Metropole and array yourself and return in less than an hour? Because, even if you can, remember that we ladies have elaborate toilets in prospect, — toilets intended for the complete prostration of the British gentry. Francesca has a yellow gown which will drive Bertie Godolphin to madness. Salemina has laid out a soft, dovelike gray and steel combination, directed towards the Church of England ; for you may not know that Sally has a vicar in her train, Mr. Beresford, and he will probably speak to-night. As for me " —

Before these shocking personalities were finished Salemina and Francesca had fled to their rooms, and Mr. Beresford took up my broken sentence and said, "As for you, Miss Hamilton, whatever gown you wear, you are sure to make one man speak, if you care about it ; but I suppose you would not listen to him unless he were English ;" and with that shot he departed.

I really think I shall have to give up the Francesca hypothesis, and, alas! I am not quite ready to adopt any other.

We discussed international marriages while we were at our toilets, Salemina and I prinking by the light of one small candle-end, while Francesca, as the youngest and prettiest, illuminated her charms with the six sitting-room candles and three filched from the little table in the hall.

I gave it as my humble opinion that for an American woman an English husband was at least an experiment; Salemina declared that for that matter a husband of any nationality was an experiment. Francesca ended the conversation flippantly by saying that in her judgment no husband at all was a much more hazardous experiment.

XII

How well I remember our last evening in Dovermarle Street!

Our large sitting-room has three long French windows, whose outside balconies are filled with potted ferns and blossoming hydrangeas. At one of these open windows sat Salemina, little Bertie Godolphin, Mrs. Beresford, the Honorable Arthur, and Francesca ; at another, as far off as possible, sat Willie Beresford and I. Mrs. Beresford had sanctioned a post-prandial cigar, for we were not going out until ten, to see, for the second time, an act of John Hare's " Pair of Spectacles."

They were talking and laughing at the other end of the room ; Mr. Beresford and I were rather quiet. (Why is it that the people with whom one loves to be silent are also the very ones with whom one loves to talk ?)

The room was dim with the light of a single lamp ; the rain had ceased ; the roar of Piccadilly came to us softened by distance. A belated vender of lavender came along the sidewalk, and as he stopped under the windows the pungent fragrance of the flowers was wafted up to us with his song.

Who 'll buy my pretty lav-ender? Sweet laven-

der, Who 'll buy my pret-ty lavender?

Sweet bloomin' lav - en - der?

The tune comes to me laden with odors. Is it not strange that the fragrances of other days steal in upon the senses together with the sights and sounds that gave them birth?

Presently a horse and cart drew up before a hotel, a little farther along, on the opposite side of the way. By the light of the street lamp under which it stopped we could see that it held a piano and two persons beside the driver. The man was masked, and wore a soft felt hat and a velvet coat. He seated himself at the

piano and played a Chopin waltz with decided sentiment and brilliancy; then,
touching the keys idly for a moment or
two, he struck a few chords of prelude
and turned towards the woman who sat
beside him. She rose, and, laying one
hand on the corner of the instrument, began to sing one of the season's favorites, —
"The Song that touched my Heart." She
also was masked, and even her figure was
hidden by a long dark cloak, the hood of
which was drawn over her head to meet
the mask. She sang so beautifully, with
such style and such feeling, it seemed in-
credible to hear her under circumstances
like these. She followed the ballad with
Händel's "Lascia ch' io pianga," which
rang out into the quiet street with almost
hopeless pathos. When she descended
from the cart to undertake the more pro-
saic occupation of passing the hat beneath the windows, I could see that she
limped slightly, and that the hand with
which she pushed back the heavy dark hair
under the hood was beautifully moulded.
They were all mystery, that couple; not
to be confounded for an instant with the

common herd of London street musicians. With what an air of the drawing-room did he of the velvet coat help the singer into the cart, and with what elegant abandon and ultra‑dilettanteism did he light a cigarette, reseat himself at the piano, and weave Scotch ballads into a charming im‑promptu! I confess I wrapped my shil‑ling in a bit of paper and dropped it over the balcony with the wish that I knew the tragedy behind this little street drama.

XIII

Willie Beresford was in a royal mood that night. You know the mood, in which the heart is so full, so full, it overruns the brim. He bought the entire stock of the lavender seller, and threw a shilling to the mysterious singer for every song she sung. He even offered to give — himself — to me! And oh! I would have taken him as gladly as ever the lavender boy took the half crown, had I been quite, quite sure of myself! A woman with a vocation ought to be still surer than other women, that it is the very jewel of love she is setting in her heart, and not a sparkling imitation. I gave myself wholly, or believed that I gave myself wholly, to art, or what I believed to be art. And is there anything more sacred than art? — Yes, one thing!

It happened something in this wise.

The singing had put us in a gentle mood, and after a long peroration from Mr. Beresford, which I do not care to repeat, I said very softly (blessing the Honorable Arthur's vociferous laughter at one of Salemina's American jokes), "But I thought perhaps it was Francesca. Are you quite sure?"

He intimated that if there were any fact in his repertory of which he was particularly and absolutely sure it was this special fact.

"It is too sudden," I objected. "Plants that blossom on shipboard" —

"This plant was rooted in American earth, and you know it, Penelope. If it chanced to blossom on the ship, it was because it had already budded on the shore; it has borne transplanting to a foreign soil, and it grows in beauty and strength every day: so no slurs, please, concerning ocean-steamer hothouses."

"I cannot say yes, yet I dare not say no; it is too soon. I must go off into the country quite by myself and think it over."

"But," urged Mr. Beresford, "you cannot think over a matter of this kind by yourself. You 'll continually be needing to refer to me for data, don't you know, on which to base your conclusions. How can you tell whether you 're in love with me or not if — (No, I am not shouting at all; it 's your guilty conscience; I 'm whispering.) How can you tell whether you 're in love with me, I repeat, unless you keep me under constant examination?"

"That seems sensible, though I dare say it is full of sophistry; but I have made up my mind to go into the country and paint while Salemina and Francesca are on the Continent. One cannot think in this whirl. A winter season in Washington followed by a summer season in London, — one wants a breath of fresh air before beginning another winter sea-

son somewhere else. Be a little patient,
please. I long for the calm that steals
over me when I am absorbed in my
brushes and my oils."

"Work is all very well," said Mr. Beresford with determination, " but I know your
habits. You have a little way of taking
your brush, and with one savage sweep
painting out a figure from your canvas.
Now if I am on the canvas of your heart,
— I say 'if' tentatively and modestly, as
becomes me, — I 've no intention of allow-
ing you to paint me out ; therefore I wish
to remain in the foreground, where I can
say 'Strike ! but hear me,' if I discover
any hostile tendencies in your eye. But
I am thankful for small favors (the 'no'
you do not quite dare say, for instance),
and I 'll talk it over with you to-morrow,
if the British gentry will give me an opportunity, and if you 'll deign to give me a
moment alone in any other place than the
Royal Academy."

"I was alone with you to-day for a
whole hour at least."

"Yes, first at the London and Westminster Bank, second in Trafalgar Square,

and third on the top of a 'bus, none of them congenial spots to a man in my humor. Penelope, you are not dull, but you don't seem to understand that I am head over " —

"What are you two people quarreling about?" cried Salemina. "Come, Penelope, get your wrap. Mrs. Beresford, is n't she charming in her new Liberty gown? If that New York wit had seen her, he could n't have said, 'If that is Liberty, give me Death!' Yes, Francesca, you must wear something over your shoulders. Whistle for two four-wheelers, Dawson, please."

PART SECOND : IN THE COUNTRY

XIV

WEST BELVERN, HOLLY HOUSE,
August, 189-.

I AM here alone. Salemina has taken
her little cloth bag and her notebook and
gone to inspect the educational and in-
dustrial methods of Germany. If she
can discover anything that they are not
already doing better in Boston, she will
take it back with her, but her state of
mind regarding the outcome of the trip
might be described as one of incredulity
tinged with hope. Francesca has accompanied Salemina. Not that the inspection of systems is much in her line, but
she prefers it to a solitude *à deux* with
me when I am in a working mood, and
she comforts herself with the anticipation
that the German army is very attractive.
Willie Beresford has gone with his mother
to Aix-les-Bains, like the dutiful son that
he is. They say, that a good son makes a
good — But that subject is dismissed to

the background for the present, for we are
in a state of armed neutrality. He has
agreed to wait until the autumn for a final
answer, and I have promised to furnish
one by that time. Meanwhile, we are to
continue our acquaintance by post, which
is a concession I would never have allowed
if I had had my wits about me.

After paying my last week's bill in
Dovermarle Street, including fees to several servants whom I knew by sight, and
several others whose acquaintance I made
for the first time at the moment of departure, I glanced at my ebbing letter of
credit and felt a season of economy setting in upon me with unusual severity; accordingly, I made an experiment of coming third class to Belvern. I handed the
guard a shilling, and he gave me a seat
riding backwards in a carriage with seven
other women, all very frumpish, but highly
respectable. As he could not possibly have
done any worse for me, I take it that he
considered the shilling a graceful tribute
to his personal charms, but as having no
other bearing whatever. The seven women stared at me throughout the journey.

When one is really of the same blood, and when one does not open one's lips or wave the stars and stripes in any possible manner, how do they detect the American? These women looked at me as if I were a highly interesting anthropoidal ape. It was not because of my attire, for I was carefully dressed down to a third-class level ; yet when I removed my plain Knox hat and leaned my head back against my traveling-pillow, an electrical shudder of intense excitement ran through the entire compartment. When I stooped to tie my shoe another current was set in motion, and when I took Charles Reade's " White Lies " from my portmanteau they glanced at one another as if to say, " Would that we could see in what language the book is written ! " As a traveling mystery I reached my highest point at Oxford, for there I purchased a small basket of plums from a boy who handed them in at the window of the carriage. After eating a few, I offered the rest to a dowdy elderly woman on my left who was munching dry biscuits from a paper bag. " What next ? " was the facial expression of the entire company. My neighbor accepted the plums, but hid them in her bag; plainly thinking them poisoned, and believing me to be a foreign conspirator, conspiring against England through the medium of her inoffensive person. In the course of the four hours' journey, I could account for the strange impression I was making only upon the theory that it is unusual to comport one's self in a first-class manner in a third-class carriage. All my companions chanced to be third class by birth as well as by ticket, and the Englishwoman who is born third class is sometimes deficient in imagination.

Upon arriving at Great Belvern (which must be pronounced " Bevern ") I took a trap, had my luggage put on in front, and started on my quest for lodgings in West Belvern, five miles distant. Several addresses had been given me by Hilda Mellifica, who has spent much time in this region, and who begged me to use her name. I told the driver that I wished to find a clean, comfortable lodging, with the view mentioned in the guide-book, and with a purple clematis over the door, if possible. The last point astounded him to such a degree that he had, I think, a serious idea of giving me into custody. (I should not be so eccentrically spontaneous with these people, if they did not feed my sense of humor by their amazement.)

We visited Holly House, Osborne, St. James, Victoria, and Albert houses, Tank Villa, Poplar Villa, Rose, Brake, and Thorn villas, as well as Hawthorn, Gorse, Fern, Shrubbery, and Providence cottages. All had apartments, but many were taken, and many more had rooms either dark and stuffy or without view. Holly House was my first stopping-place. Why will a woman voluntarily call her place by a name which she can never pronounce? It is my landlady's misfortune that she is named 'Obbs, and mine that I am called 'Amilton, but Mrs. 'Obbs must have rushed with eyes wide open on 'Olly 'Ouse. I found sitting-room and bedroom at Holly House for two guineas a week; everything, except roof, extra. This was more than, in my new spirit of economy, I desired to pay, but after exhausting my list I was obliged to go back rather than sleep in the highroad. Mrs. Hobbs offered to deduct two shillings a week if I stayed until Christmas, and said she should not charge me a penny for the linen. Thanking her with tears in my eyes, I requested dinner. There was no meat in the house, so I supped frugally off two boiled eggs, a stodgy household loaf, and a mug of ale, after which I climbed the stairs, and retired to my feather bed in a rather depressed frame of mind.

XV

Visions of Salemina and Francesca driving under the linden-trees in Berlin flitted across my troubled reveries, with glimpses of Willie Beresford and his mother at Aix-les-Bains. At this distance and in the dead of night, my sacrifice in coming here seemed fruitless. Why did I not allow myself to drift forever on that pleasant sea which has been lapping me in sweet and indolent content these many weeks? Of what use to labor, to struggle, to deny myself, for an art to which I can never be more than the humblest handmaiden? I felt like crying out, as did once a braver woman's soul than mine, "Let me be weak! I have been seeming to be strong so many years!" The woman and the artist in me have always struggled for the mastery. So far the artist has triumphed, and now all at once the woman is uppermost. I should think the two ought to be able to live peaceably in the same tenement; they do manage it in some cases; but it seems a law of my being that I shall either be all one or all the other.

The question for me to ask myself now is, "Am I in love with loving and with being loved, or am I in love with Willie Beresford?" How many women have confounded the two, I wonder?

In this mood I fell asleep, and on a sudden I found myself in a dear New England garden. The pillow slipped away, and my cheek pressed a fragrant mound of mignonette, the selfsame one on which I hid my tear-stained face and sobbed my heart out in childish grief and longing for the mother who would never hold me again. The moon came up over

the Belvern Hills and shone on my half-
closed lids ; but to me it was a very different moon, the far-away moon of my childhood, with a river rippling beneath its
silver rays.   And the wind that rustled
among the poplar branches outside my
window was, in my dream, stirring the
pink petals of a blossoming apple-tree
that used to grow beside the bank of
mignonette, wafting down sweet odors
and drinking in sweeter ones.   And presently there stole in upon this harmony of
enchanting sounds and delicate fragrances,
in which childhood and womanhood, pleasure and pain, memory and anticipation,
seemed strangely intermingled, the faint
music of a voice, growing clearer and
clearer as my ear became familiar with
its cadences.   And what the dream voice
said to me was something like this : —

" If thou wouldst have happiness, choose
neither fame, which doth not long abide,
nor power, which stings the hand that
wields it, nor gold, which glitters but
never glorifies ; but choose thou Love,
and hold it forever in thy heart of hearts ;
for Love is the purest and the mightiest

force in the universe, and once it is thine all other gifts shall be added unto thee. Love that is passionate yet reverent, tender yet strong, selfish in desiring all yet generous in giving all; love of man for woman and woman for man, of parent for child and friend for friend, — when this is born in the soul, the desert blossoms as the rose. Straightway new hopes and wishes, sweet longings and pure ambitions, spring into being, like green shoots that lift their tender heads in sunny places; and if the soil be kind, they grow stronger and more beautiful as each glad day laughs in the rosy skies. And by and by singing birds come and build their nests in the branches; and these are the pleasures of life. And the birds sing not often, because of a serpent that lurketh in the garden. And the name of the serpent is Satiety. He maketh the heart to grow weary of what it once danced and leaped to think upon, and the ear to wax dull to the melody of sounds that once were sweet, and the eye blind to the beauty that once led enchantment captive. And sometimes, — we know not why, but we shall know hereafter, for life is not completely happy since it is not heaven, nor completely unhappy since it is the road thither, — sometimes the light of the sun is withdrawn for a moment, and that which is fairest vanishes from the place that was enriched by its presence. Yet the garden is never quite deserted. Modest flowers, whose charms we had not noted when youth was bright and the world seemed ours, now lift their heads in sheltered places and whisper peace. The morning song of the birds is hushed, for the dawn breaks less rosily in the eastern skies, but at twilight they still come and nestle in the branches that were sunned in the smile of love and watered with its happy tears. And over the grave of each buried hope or joy stands an angel with strong comforting hands and patient smile; and the name of the garden is Life, and the angel is Memory."

XVI

NORTH BELVERN.
At Mrs. Bobby's cottage.

I have changed my Belvern, and there are so many others left to choose from that I might live in a different Belvern each week. North, South, East, and West Belvern, New Belvern, Old Belvern, Great Belvern, Little Belvern, Belvern Link, Belvern Common, and Belvern Wells. They are all nestled together in the velvet hollows or on the wooded crowns of the matchless Belvern Hills, from which they look down upon the fairest plains that ever blessed the eye. One can see from their heights a score of market towns and villages, three splendid cathedrals, each in a different county, the queenly Severn winding like a silver thread among the trees, with soft-flowing Avon and gentle Teme watering the verdant meadows through which they pass. All these hills and dales were once the Royal Forest, and afterwards thé Royal Chase, of Belvern, covering nearly seven thousand acres in three counties; and from the lonely height of the Beacon no less than

"Twelve fair counties saw the blaze"

of signals, when the country was threatened by a Spanish invasion. As for me, I mourn the decay of Romance with a great R; we have it still among us, but we spell it with a smaller letter. It must be so much more interesting to be threatened with an invasion, especially a Spanish invasion, than with a strike, for instance. The clashing of swords and the flashing of spears in the sunshine are so much more dazzling and inspiring than a line of policemen with clubs! Yes, I wish it were the age of chivalry again, and that I were looking down from these hills into the Royal Chase. Of course I know that there were wicked and selfish tyrants in those days, before the free press, the jury system, and the folding-bed had wrought their beneficent influences upon the common mind and heart. Of course they would have sneered at Browning Societies and improved tenements, and of course they did not care a

penny whether woman had the ballot or
not, so long as man had the bottle ; but I
would that the other moderns were enjoy-
ing the modern improvements, and that I
were gazing into the cool depths of those
deep forests where there were once good
lairs for the wolf and wild boar.   I should
like to hear the baying of the hounds and
the mellow horns of the huntsman.   I
should like to see the royal cavalcade
emerging from one of those wooded
glades : monarch and baron bold, proud
prelate, abbot and prior, belted knight
and ladye fair, sweeping in gorgeous array
under the arcades of the overshadowing
trees, silver spurs and jeweled trappings
glittering in the sunlight, princely forms
bending low over the saddles of the court
beauties.   Why, oh why, is it not possible
to be picturesque and pious in the same
epoch ?   Why may not chivalry and charity go hand in hand?   It amuses me to
imagine the amazement of the barons,
bold and belted knights, could they be re-
suscitated for a sufficient length of time to
gaze upon the hydropathic establishments
which dot their ancient hunting-grounds.

It would have been very difficult to interest the age of chivalry in hydropathy.

Such is the fascination of historic as-
sociation that I am sure, if I could drag
my beloved but conscientious Salemina
from some foreign soup kitchen which she
is doubtless inspecting, I could make even
her mourn the vanished past with me this
morning, on the Beacon's towering head.
For Salemina wearies of the age of charity
sometimes, as every one does who is trying
to make it a beautiful possibility.

XVII

The manner of my changing from West
to North Belvern was this. When I had
been two days at Holly House, I reflected
that my sitting-room faced the wrong way
for the view, and that my bedroom was
dark and not large enough to swing a cat
in. Not that there was the remotest necessity of my swinging cats in it, but the
figure of speech is always useful. Neither
did I care to occupy myself with the peren-
nial inspection and purchase of raw edibles,
when I wished to live in an ideal world

and paint a great picture. Mrs. Hobbs
would come to my bedside in the morning
and ask me if I would like to buy a fowl.
When I looked upon the fowl, limp in
death, with its headless neck hanging de-
jectedly over the edge of the plate, its
giblets and kidneys lying in immodest
confusion on the outside of itself, and its
liver " tucked under its wing, poor thing,"
I never wanted to buy it. But one morning, in taking my walk, I chanced upon
an idyllic spot : the front of the whitewashed cottage embowered in flowers,
bird-cages built into these bowers, a little
notice saying " Canaries for Sale," and an
English rose of a baby sitting in the path
stringing hollyhock buds. There was no
apartment sign, but I walked in, ostensibly
to buy some flowers. I met Mrs. Bobby,
loved her at first sight, the passion was
reciprocal, and I wheedled her into giving
me her own sitting-room and the bedroom
above it. It only remained now for me
to break my projected change of residence
to my present landlady, and this I distinctly dreaded.• Of course Mrs. Hobbs
said, when I timidly mentioned the sub-

ject, that she wished she had known I was leaving an hour before, for she had just refused a lady and her husband, most desirable persons, who looked as if they would be permanent. Can it be that lodgers radiate the permanent or transitory quality, quite unknown to themselves?

I was very much embarrassed, as she threatened to become tearful; and as I was determined never to give up Mrs. Bobby, I said desperately, "I must leave you, Mrs. Hobbs, I must indeed; but as you seem to feel so badly about it, I'll go out and find you another lodger in my place."

The fact is, I had seen, not long before, a lady going in and out of houses, as I had done on the night of my arrival, and it occurred to me that I might pursue her, and persuade her to take my place in Holly House and buy the headless fowl. I walked for nearly an hour before I was rewarded with a glimpse of my victim's gray dress whisking round the corner of Pump Street. I approached, and, with a smile that was intended to be a justification in itself, I explained my somewhat

" I loved her at first sight "

unusual mission. She was rather unreceptive at first ; she thought evidently that I was to have a percentage on her, if I succeeded in capturing her alive and delivering her to Mrs. Hobbs ; but she was very weary and discouraged, and finally fell in with my plans. She accompanied me home, was introduced to Mrs. Hobbs, and engaged my rooms from the following day. As she had a sister, she promised to be a more lucrative incumbent than I ; she enjoyed ordering food in a raw state, did not care for views, and thought purple clematis vines only a shelter for insects : so every one was satisfied, and I most of all when I wrestled with Mrs. Hobbs's itemized bill for two nights and one day. Her weekly account must be rolled on a cylinder, I should think, like the list of Don Juan's amours, for the bill of my brief residence beneath her roof was quite three feet in length, each of the following items being set down every twenty-four hours : —

    Apartments.
    Ale.
    Bath.
    Kidney beans.

Candles.
Vegetable marrow.
Tea.
Eggs.
Butter.
Bread.
Cut off joint.
Plums.
Potatoes.
Chops.
Kipper.
Rasher.
Salt.
Pepper.
Vinegar.
Sugar.
Washing towels.
Lights.
Kitchen fire.
Sitting-room fire.
Attendance.
Boots.

The total was seventeen shillings and sixpence, and as Mrs. Hobbs wrote upon it, in her neat English hand, " Received payment, with respectful thanks," and applied the usual penny stamp, she remarked casually that service was not included in " attendance," but that she would leave the amount to me.

XVIII

Mrs. Bobby and I were born for each other, though we have been a long time in coming together. She is the pink of neatness and cheeriness, and she has a broad, comfortable bosom on which one might lay a motherless head, if one felt lonely in a stranger land. No raw fowls visit my bedside here ; food comes as I wish it to come when I am painting, like manna from heaven. Mrs. Bobby brings me three times a day something to eat, and though it is always whatever she likes, I always agree in her choice, and send the blue dishes away empty. She asked me this morning if I enjoyed my " h'egg," and remarked that she had only one fowl, but it laid an egg for me every morning, so I might know it was "fresh as fresh." It is certainly convenient : the fowl lays the egg from seven to seven thirty, I eat it from eight to eight thirty ; no haste, no waste. Never before have I seen such heavenly harmony between supply and demand. Never before have I been in such visible and unbroken connection with

the source of my food. If I should ever
desire two eggs, or if the fowl should turn
sulky or indolent, I suppose Mrs. Bobby
would have to go half a mile to the nearest
shop, but as yet everything has worked to
a charm. The cow is milked into my
pitcher in the morning, and the fowl lays
her egg almost literally in my egg-cup.
One of the little Bobbies pulls a kidney
bean or a tomato or digs a potato for my
dinner, about half an hour before it is
served. There is a sheep in the garden,
but I hardly think it supplies the chops;
those, at least, are not raised on the
premises.

One grievance I did have at first, but
Mrs. Bobby removed the thorn from the
princess' pillow as soon as it was mentioned. Our next-door neighbor had a
kennel of homesick, discontented, and
sleepless puppies of various breeds, that
were in the habit of howling all night
until Mrs. Bobby expostulated with Mrs.
Gooch in my behalf. She told me that
she found Mrs. Gooch very snorty, very
snorty indeed, because the pups were an
'obby of her 'usbant's ; whereupon Mrs.

Bobby responded that if Mrs. Gooch's 'usbant 'ad to 'ave an 'obby, it was a shame it 'ad to be 'owling pups to keep h'innocent people awake o' nights. The puppies were removed, but I almost felt guilty at finding fault with a dog in this country. It is a matter of constant surprise to me, and it always gives me a warm glow in the region of the heart, to see the supremacy of the dog in England. He is respected, admired, loved, and considered, as he deserves to be everywhere, but as he frequently is not. He is admitted on all excursions; he is taken into the country for his health; he is a factor in all the master's plans; in short, the English dog is a member of the family, in good and regular standing.

My interior surroundings are all charming. My little sitting-room, out of which I turned Mrs. Bobby, is bright with potted ferns and flowering plants, and on its walls, besides the photographs of a large and unusually plain family, I have two works of art which inspire me anew every time I gaze at them : the first, a Scriptural subject, treated by an enthusiastic but inexperienced hand, " Susanne dans le Bain, surprise par les Deux Vieillards ; " the second, " The White Witch of Worcester on her Way to the Stake at High Cross." The unfortunate lady in the latter picture is attired in a white lawn wrapper with angel sleeves, and is followed by an abbess with prayer-book, and eight surpliced choir-boys with candles. I have been long enough in England to understand the significance of the candles. Doubtless the White Witch had paid four shillings a week for each of them in her prison lodging, and she naturally wished to burn them to the end.

One has no need, though, of pictures on the walls here, for the universe seems unrolled at one's very feet. As I look out of my window the last thing before I go to sleep, I see the lights of Great Belvern, the dim shadows of the distant cathedral towers, the quaint priory seven centuries old, and just the outline of Holly Bush Hill, a sacred seat of magic science where the Druids investigated the secrets of the stars, and sought, by auspices and sacrifices, to forecast the future and to penetrate the designs of the gods.

It makes me feel very new, very un-
developed, to look out of that window.
If I were an Englishwoman, say the fifty-
fifth duchess of something, I could easily
glow with pride to think that I was part
and parcel of such antiquity; the fortunate heiress not only of land and titles,
but of historic associations. But as I am
an American with a very recent background, I blow out my candle with the
feeling that it is rather grand to be making history for somebody else to inherit.

XIX

I am almost too comfortable with Mrs.
Bobby. In fact, I wished to be just a little
miserable in Belvern, so that I could paint
with a frenzy. Sometimes, when I have
been in a state of almost despairing loneliness and gloom, the colors have glowed on
my canvas and the lines have shaped themselves under my hand independent of my
own volition. Now, tucked away in a
corner of my consciousness is the knowledge that I need never be lonely again
unless I choose. When I yield myself

fully to the sweet enchantment of this
thought, I feel myself in the mood to
paint sunshine, flowers, and happy children's faces; yet I am sadly lacking in
concentration, all the same. The fact is,
I am no artist in the true sense of the
word. My hope flies ever in front of my
best success, and that momentary success
does not deceive me in the very least. I
know exactly how much, or rather how
little, I am worth; that I lack the imagination, the industry, the training, the
ambition, to achieve any lasting results.
I have the artistic temperament in so far
that it is impossible for me to work merely
for money or popularity, or indeed for anything less than the desire to express the
best that is in me without fear or favor.
It would never occur to me to trade on
present approval and dash off unworthy
stuff while I have command of the market. I am quite above all that, but I am
distinctly below that other mental and
spiritual level where art is enough; where
pleasure does not signify; where one shuts
one's self up and produces from sheer necessity; where one is compelled by relent-

less law ; where sacrifice does not count ;
where ideas throng the brain and plead
for release in expression ; where effort is
joy, and the prospect of doing something
enduring lures the soul on to new and
ever new endeavor : so I shall never be
rich or famous.

What shall I paint to-day ? Shall it be
the bit of garden underneath my window,
with the tangle of pinks and roses, and
the cabbages growing appetizingly beside
the sweet-williams, the woodbine climbing
over the brown stone wall, the wicket gate,
and the cherry-tree with its fruit hanging
red against the whitewashed cottage ?
Ah, if I could only paint it so truly that
you could hear the drowsy hum of the
bees among the thyme, and smell the
scented hay-meadows in the distance, and
feel that it is midsummer in England !
That would indeed be truth, and that
would be art. Shall I paint the Bobby
baby as he stoops to pick the cowslips
and the flax, his head as yellow and his
eyes as blue as the flowers themselves ;
or that bank opposite the gate, with its
gorse bushes in golden bloom, its moun-

tain ash hung with scarlet berries, its tufts of harebells blossoming in the crevices of rock, and the quaint low clock tower at the foot? Can I not paint all these in the full glow of summer-time, and paint them all the better because it is summer-time in my secret heart whenever I open the door a bit and admit its life-giving warmth and beauty? I think I can, if I can only quit dreaming.

I wonder how the great artists worked, and under what circumstances they threw aside the implements of their craft, impatient of all but the throb of life itself? Could Raphael paint Madonnas the week of his betrothal? Did Thackeray write a chapter the day his daughter was born? Did Plato philosophize freely when he was in love? Were there interruptions in the world's great revolutions, histories, dramas, reforms, poems, and marbles when their creators fell for a brief moment under the spell of the little blind tyrant who makes slaves of us all? It must have been so. Your chronometer heart, on whose pulsations you can reckon as on the procession of the equinoxes, never gave anything to the world unless it were a system of diet, or something quite uncolored and unglorified by the imagination.

XX

There are many donkeys owned in these nooks among the hills, and some of the thriftier families keep donkey-chairs (or "cheers," as they call them) to let to the casual summer visitor. This vehicle is a regular Bath chair, into which the donkey is harnessed. Some of them have a tiny driver's seat, where a small lad sits beating and berating the donkey for the incumbent, generally a decrepit dowager from London. Other chairs are minus this absurd coachman's perch, and in this sort I take my daily drives. I hire the miniature chariot from an old woman who dwells at the top of Gorse Hill, and who charges one and fourpence the hour. (A little more when she fetches the donkey to the door, or when the weather is wet, or the day is very warm, or there is an unusual breeze blowing, or I wish to go round the hills; but under ordinary circumstances, which may at any time occur, but which never do, one and four the hour. It is only a shilling, if you have the boy to drive you; but of course, if you drive yourself, you throw the boy out of employment, and have to pay extra.)

It was in this fashion and on these elastic terms that I first met you, Jane, and this chapter shall be sacred to you! Jane the long-eared, Jane the iron-jawed, Jane the stubborn, Jane donkier than other donkeys, — in a word, *mulier!* It may be that Jane has made her bow to the public before this. If she has ever come into close relation with man or woman possessed of the instinct of self-expression, then this is certainly not her first appearance in print, for no human being could know Jane and fail to mention her.

Pause, Jane, — this you will do gladly, I am sure, since pausing is the one accomplishment to which you lend yourself with special energy, — pause, Jane, while I sing a canticle to your character. Jane is a tiny — person, I was about to say, for she has so strong an individuality that I can scarcely think of her as less than human — Jane is a tiny, solemn creature, looking all docility and decorum, with long hair of a subdued tan color, very much worn off in patches, I fear, by the offending toe of man.

I am a member of the Society for the Prevention of Cruelty to Animals, and I hope that I am as tender-hearted as most women; nevertheless, I can understand how a man of weak principle and violent temper, or a man possessed of a desire to get to a particular spot not favored by Jane, or by a wish to reach any spot by a certain hour, — I can understand how such a man, carried away by helpless wrath, might possibly ruffle Jane's sad-colored hair with the toe of his boot.

Jane is small, yet mighty. She is *multum in parvo;* she is the rock of Gibraltar in animate form; she is cosmic obstinacy on four legs. When following out the devices and desires of her own heart, or resisting the devices and desires of yours, she can put a pressure of five hundred tons on the bit. She is further fortified by the possession of legs which have iron rods concealed in them, these iron rods

terminating in stout grip-hooks, with which
she takes hold on mother earth with an
expression that seems to say, —

> "This rock shall fly
> From its firm base
> As soon as I."

When I start out in the afternoon, Mrs.
Bobby frequently asks me where I am
going. I always answer that I have not
made up my mind, though what I really
mean to say is that Jane has not made up
her mind. She never makes up her mind
until after I have made up mine, lest by
some unhappy accident she might choose
the very excursion that I desire myself.

XXI

For example, I wish to visit St. Bridget's
Well, concerning which there are some
quaint old verses in a village history :—

> "Out of thy famous hille,
> There daylie springyeth,
> A water passynge stille,
> That alwayes bringyeth
> Grete comfort to all them
> That are diseased men,
> And makes them well again
> To prayse the Lord."

" Hast thou a wound to heale,
The wyche doth greve thee;
Come thenn unto this welle;
It will relieve thee;
Nolie me tangeries,
And other maladies,
Have there theyr remedies,
    Prays'd be the Lord."

St. Bridget's Well is a beautiful spot, and my desire to see it is a perfectly laudable one. In strict justice, it is really no concern of Jane whether my wishes are laudable or not; but it only makes the case more flagrant when she interferes with the reasonable plans of a reasonable being. Never since the day we first met have I harbored a thought that I wished to conceal from Jane (would that she could say as much!); nevertheless she treats me as if I were a monster of caprice. As I said before, I wish to visit St. Bridget's Well, but Jane absolutely refuses to take me there. After we pass Belvern churchyard we approach two roads: the one to the right leads to the Holy Well; the one to the left leads to Shady Dell Farm, where Jane lived when she was a girl. At the critical moment I pull the right rein with all my force. In vain : Jane is always overcome by sentiment when she sees that left-hand road. She bears to the left like a whirlwind, and nothing can stop her mad career until she is again amid the scenes so dear to her recollection, the beloved pastures where the mother still lives at whose feet she brayed in early youth !

Now this is all very pretty and touching. Her action has, in truth, its springs in a most commendable sentiment that I should be the last to underrate. Shady Dell Farm is interesting, too, for once, if one can swallow one's wrath and dudgeon at being taken there against one's will; and one feels that Jane's parents and Jane's early surroundings must be worth a single visit, if they could produce a donkey of such unusual capacity. Still, she must know, if she knows anything, that a person does not come from America and pay one and fourpence the hour (or thereabouts) merely in order to visit the home of her girlhood, which is neither mentioned in Baedeker nor set down in the local guide-books as a feature of interest.

Whether, in addition to her affection
for Shady Dell Farm, she has an objec-
tion to St. Bridget's Well, and thus is
strengthened by a double motive, I do
not know. She may consider it a relic of
popish superstition; she may be a Pro-
testant donkey; she is a Dissenter, —
there 's no doubt about that.

But, you ask, have you tried various
methods of bringing her to terms and
gaining your own desires? Certainly. I
have coaxed, beaten, prodded, prayed. I
have tried leading her past the Shady
Dell turn; she walks all over my feet, and
then starts for home, I running behind
until I can catch up with her. I have
offered her one and tenpence the hour;
she remained firm. One morning I had a
happy inspiration; I determined on con-
quering Jane by a subterfuge. I said to
myself: "I am going to start for St.
Bridget's Well, as usual; several yards
before we reach the two roads, I shall begin pulling, not the right, but the left rein.
Jane will lift her ears suddenly and say
to herself: ' What! has this girl fallen in
love with my birthplace at last, and does

she now prefer it to St. Bridget's Well?
Then she shall not have it!' Whereupon
Jane will start madly down the right-hand
road for the first time, I pulling steadily
at the left rein to keep up appearances,
and I shall at last realize my wishes."

This was my inspiration. Would you
believe that it failed utterly? It should
have succeeded and would with an ordinary donkey, but Jane saw through it.
She obeyed my pull on the left rein, and
went to Shady Dell Farm as usual.

Another of Jane's eccentricities is a
violent aversion to perambulators. As
Belvern is a fine, healthy, growing country,
with steadily increasing population, the
roads are naturally alive with perambulators; or at least alive with the babies
inside the perambulators. These are the
more alarming to the timid eye in that
many of them are double-barreled, so to
speak, and are loaded to the muzzle with
babies; for not only do Belvern babies
frequently appear as twins, but there are
often two youngsters of a perambulator
age in the same family at the same time.
To weave that donkey and that Bath

" cheer " through the narrow streets of the various Belverns without putting to death any babies, and without engendering the outspoken condemnation of the screaming mothers and nursery maids, is a task for a Jehu. Of course Jane makes it more difficult by lunging into one perambulator in avoiding another, but she prefers even that risk to the degradation of treading the path I wish her to tread.

I often wish that for one brief moment I might remove the lid of Jane's brain and examine her mental processes. She would not exasperate me so deeply if I could be certain of her springs of action. Is she old, is she rheumatic, is she lazy, is she hungry? Sometimes I think she means well, and is only ignorant and dull ; but this hypothesis grows less and less tenable as I know her better. Sometimes I conclude that she does not understand me ; the difference in nationality may trouble her. If an Englishman cannot understand an American woman all at once, why should an English donkey? Perhaps it takes an American donkey to comprehend an American woman. Yet I cannot bring myself to drive any other donkey ; I am always hoping to impress myself on her imagination, and conquer her will through her fancy. Meanwhile, I like to feel myself in the grasp of a nature stronger than my own, and so I hold to Jane, and buy a photograph of St. Bridget's Well !

XXII

It was about two o'clock in the afternoon, and I suddenly heard a strange sound, that of our fowl cackling. Yesterday I heard her telltale note about noon, and the day before just as I was eating my breakfast. I knew that it would be so ! The serpent has entered Eden. That fowl has laid before eight in the morning for three weeks without interruption, and she has now entered upon a career of wild and reckless uncertainty which compels me to eat eggs from twelve to twenty-four hours old, just as if I were in London.

> Alas for the rarity
> Of regularity
> Under the sun !

A hen, being of the feminine gender,

underestimates the majesty of order and system ; she resents any approach to the unimaginative monotony of the machine. Probably the Confederated Fowl Union has been meddling with our little paradise where Labor and Capital have dwelt in heavenly unity until now. Nothing can be done about it, of course ; even if it were possible to communicate with the fowl, she would say, I suppose, that she would lay when she was ready, and not before ; at least, that is what an American hen would say.

Just as I was brooding over these mysteries and trying to hatch out some conclusions, Mrs. Bobby knocked at the door, and, coming in, courtesied very low before saying, " It 's about namin' the 'ouse, miss."

"Oh, yes. Pray don't stand, Mrs. Bobby; take a chair. I am not very busy ; I am only painting prickles on my gorse bushes, so we will talk it over."

I shall not attempt to give you Mrs. Bobby's dialect, in reporting my various interviews with her, for the spelling of it is quite beyond my powers. Pray remove all the *h*'s wherever they occur, and insert them where they do not; but there will be, over and beyond this, an intonation quite impossible to render.

Mrs. Bobby bought her place only a few months ago, for she lived in Cheltenham before Mr. Bobby died. The last incumbent had probably been of Welsh extraction, for the cottage had been named "Dan - y - Cefn." Mrs. Bobby declared, however, that she would n't have a heathenish name posted on her house, and expect her friends to pronounce it when she could n't pronounce it herself. She seemed grieved when at first I could not see the absolute necessity of naming the cottage at all, telling her that in America we named only grand places. She was struck dumb with amazement at this piece of information, and failed to conceive of the confusion that must ensue in villages where streets were scarcely named or houses numbered. I confess it had never occurred to me that our manner of doing was highly inconvenient, if not impossible, and I approached the subject of the name with more interest and more modesty.

"Well, Mrs. Bobby," I began, "it is to be Cottage; we 've decided that, have we not? It is to be Cottage, not House, Lodge, Mansion, or Villa. We cannot name it after any flower that blows, because they are all taken. Have all the trees been used?"

"Thank you, miss, yes, miss, all but h'ash-tree, and we 'ave no h'ash."

"Very good, we must follow another plan. Family names seem to be chosen, such as Gower House, Marston Villa, and the like. 'Bobby Cottage,' is not pretty. What was your maiden name, Mrs. Bobby?"

"Buggins, thank you, miss, 'Elizabeth Buggins, Licensed to sell Poultry,' was my name and title when I met Mr. Bobby."

"I 'm sorry, but 'Buggins Cottage' is still more impossible than 'Bobby Cottage.' Now here 's another idea: where were you born, Mrs. Bobby?"

"In Snitterfield, thank you, miss."

"Dear, dear! how unserviceable!"

"Thank you, miss."

"Where was Mr. Bobby born?"

"He never mentioned, miss."

(Mr. Bobby must have been expansive, for they were married twenty years.)

"There is always Victoria or Albert," I said tentatively, as I wiped my brushes.

"Yes, miss, but with all respect to her Majesty, them names give me a turn when I see them on the gates, I am that sick of them."

"True. Can we call it anything that will suggest its situation? Is there a Hill Crest?"

"Yes, miss, there is 'Ill Crest, 'Ill Top, 'Ill View, 'Ill Side, 'Ill End, H'under 'Ill, 'Ill Bank, and 'Ill Terrace."

"I should think that would do for Hill."

"Thank you, miss. 'Ow would 'The 'Edge' do, miss?"

"But we have no hedge." (She shall not have anything with an *h* in it, if I can help it.)

"No, miss, but I thought I might set out a bit, if worst come to worst."

"And wait three or four years before people would know why the cottage was named? Oh, no, Mrs. Bobby."

"Thank you, miss."

"We might have something quite out

of the common, like 'Providence Cottage,' down the bank. I don't know why Mrs. Jones calls it Providence Cottage, unless she thinks it's a providence that she has one at all ; or because, as it's right on the edge of the hill, she thinks it's a providence that it has n't blown off. How would you like 'Peace' or 'Rest' Cottage ?"

" Begging your pardon, miss, it's neither peace nor rest I gets in it these days, with a twenty - five pound debt 'anging over me, and three children to feed and clothe."

" I fear we are not very clever, Mrs. Bobby, or we should hit upon the right thing with less trouble. I know what I will do : I will go down in the road and look at the place for a long time from the outside, and try to think what it suggests to me."

" Thank you, miss ; and I 'm sure I 'm grateful for all the trouble you are taking with my small affairs."

Down I went, and leaned over the wicket gate, gazing at the unnamed cottage. The bricked pathway was scrubbed

as clean as a penny, and the stone step
and the floor of the little kitchen as well.
The garden was a maze of fragrant bloom,
with never a weed in sight. The fowl
cackled cheerily still, adding insult to in-
jury, the pet sheep munched grass con-
tentedly, and the canaries sang in their
cages under the vines. Mrs. Bobby settled herself on the porch with a pan of
peas in her neat gingham lap, and all at
once I cried : —

"'Comfort Cottage'! It is the very
essence of comfort, Mrs. Bobby, even if
there is not absolute peace or rest. Let
me paint the signboard for you this very
day."

Mrs. Bobby was most complacent over
the name. She had the greatest confidence in my judgment, and the charac-
terization pleased her housewifely pride,
so much so that she flushed with pleasure
as she said that if she 'ad 'er 'ealth she
thought she could keep the place looking
so that the passers-by would easily h'understand the name.

XXIII

It was some days after the naming of
the cottage that Mrs. Bobby admitted me
into her financial secrets, and explained
the difficulties that threatened her peace
of mind. She still has twenty-five pounds
to pay before Comfort Cottage is really
her own. With her cow and her vegetable garden, to say nothing of her pro-
crastinating fowl, she manages to eke out
a frugal existence, now that her eldest son
is in a blacksmith's shop at Worcester and
is sending her part of his weekly savings.
But it has been a poor season for canaries,
and a still poorer one for lodgers ; for people in these degenerate days prefer to be
nearer the hotels and the mild gayeties of
the larger settlements. It is all very well
so long as I remain with her, and she
wishes fervently that that may be forever ; for never, she says eloquently, never
in all her Cheltenham and Belvern experience, has she encountered such a jewel
of a lodger as her dear Miss 'Amilton, so
little trouble, and always a bit of praise
for her plain cooking, and a pleasant word

for the children, to whom most lodgers object, and such an interest in the cow and the fowl and the garden and the canaries, and such kindness in painting the name of the cottage, so that it is the finest thing in the village, and nobody can get past the 'ouse without stopping to gape at it! But when her American lodger leaves her, she asks,—and who is she that can expect to keep a beautiful young lady who will be naming her own cottage and painting signboards for herself before long, likely?—but when her American lodger is gone, how is she, Mrs. Bobby, to put by a few shillings a month towards the debt on the cottage? These are some of the problems she presents to me. I have turned them over and over in my mind as I have worked, and even asked Willie Beresford in my weekly letter what he could suggest. Of course he could not suggest anything; men never can. All at once, one morning, a happy idea struck me, and I ran down to Mrs. Bobby, who was weeding the onion bed in the back garden.

"Mrs. Bobby," I said, sitting down

comfortably on the edge of the lettuce-frame, "I am sure I know how you can earn many a shilling during the summer and autumn months, and you must begin the experiment while I am here to advise you. I want you to serve five o'clock tea in your garden."

"But, miss, thanking you kindly, nobody would think of stoppin' 'ere for a cup of tea once in a twelvemonth."

"You never know what people will do until you try them. People will do almost anything, Mrs. Bobby, if you only put it into their heads, and this is the way we shall make our suggestion to the public. I will paint a second signboard to hang below 'Comfort Cottage.' It will be much more beautiful than the other, for it shall have a steaming kettle on it, and a cup and saucer, and the words 'Tea Served Here' underneath, the letters all intertwined with tea plants. I don't know how tea plants look, but then neither does the public. You will set one round table on the porch, so that if it threatens rain, as it sometimes does, you know, in England, people will not be afraid to sit down; and the other you will put under the yew-tree near the gate. The tables must be immaculate; no spotted, rumpled cloths and chipped cups at Comfort Cottage, which is to be a strictly first-class tea station. You will put vases of flowers on the tables, and you will not mix red, yellow, purple, and blue ones in the same vase" —

"It 's the way the good Lord mixes 'em in the fields," interjected Mrs. Bobby piously.

"Very likely; but you will permit me to remark that the good Lord can manage things successfully which we poor humans cannot. You will set out your cream jug that was presented to Mrs. Martha Buggins by her friends and neighbors as a token of respect in 1823, and the bowl that was presented to Mr. Bobby as a sword and shooting prize in 1860, and all your pretty little odds and ends. You will get everything ready in the kitchen, so that customers won't have to wait long; but you will not prepare much in advance, so that there 'll be nothing wasted."

"It sounds beautiful in your mouth,

miss, and it surely would n't be any 'arm to make a trial of it."

"Of course it won't. There is no inn here where nice people will stop (who would ever think of asking for tea at The Retired Soldier?), and the moment they see our sign, in walking or driving past, that moment they will be consumed with thirst. You do not begin to appreciate our advantages as a tea station. In the first place, there is a watering-trough not far from the gate, and drivers very often stop to water their horses ; then we have the lovely garden which everybody admires ; and if everything else fails, there is the baby. Put that faded pink flannel slip on Jem, showing his tanned arms and legs as usual, tie up his sleeves with blue bows as you did last Sunday, put my white tennis cap on the back of his yellow curls, turn him loose in the hollyhocks, and await results. Did I not open the gate the moment I saw him, though there was no apartment sign in the window?"

Mrs. Bobby was overcome by the magic of my arguments, and as there were positively no attendant risks, we decided on

an early opening. The very next day
after the hanging of the second sign, I
superintended the arrangements myself.
It was a nice thirsty afternoon, and as I
filled the flower vases I felt such a desire
for custom and such a love of trade ani-
mating me that I was positively ashamed.
At three o'clock I went upstairs and threw
myself on the bed for a nap, for I had
been sketching on the hills since early
morning. It may have been an hour later
when I heard the sound of voices and the
stopping of a heavy vehicle before the
house. I stole to the front window, and,
peeping under the shelter of the vines,
saw a char-a-bancs, on the way from Great
Belvern to the Beacon. It held three gentlemen, two ladies, and four children, and
everything had worked precisely as I intended. The driver had seen the watering-trough, the gentlemen had seen the
tea sign, the children had seen the flowers
and the canaries, and the ladies had seen
the baby. I went to the back window to
call an encouraging word to Mrs. Bobby,
but to my horror I saw that worthy woman disappearing at the extreme end of

the lane in full chase of our cow, that had broken down the fence, and was now at large, with some of our neighbor's turnip tops hanging from her mouth.

XXIV

Ruin stared us in the face. Were our cherished plans to be frustrated by a marauding cow, who little realized that she was imperiling her own means of existence? Were we to turn away three, five, nine thirsty customers at one fell swoop? Never! None of these people ever saw me before, nor would ever see me again. What was to prevent my serving them with tea? I had on a pink cotton gown, — that was well enough; I hastily buttoned on a clean painting-apron, and seizing a freshly laundered cushion cover lying on the bureau, a square of lace and embroidery, I pinned it on my hair for a cap while descending the stairs. Everything was right in the kitchen, for Mrs. Bobby had flown in the midst of her preparations. The loaf, the bread knife, the butter, the marmalade, all stood on the table, and the kettle was boiling. I set the tea to draw, and then dashed to the door, bowed appetizingly to the visitors, showed them to the tables with a winning smile (which was to be extra), seated the children maternally on the steps and laid napkins before them, dashed back to the kitchen, cut the thin bread and butter, and brought it with the marmalade, asked my customers if they desired cream and told them it was extra, went back and brought a tray with tea, boiling water, milk, and cream. Lowering my voice to an English sweetness, and dropping a few *h*'s ostentatiously as I answered questions, I poured five cups of tea, and four mugs for the children, and cut more bread and butter, for they were all eating like wolves. They praised the butter. I told them it was a specialty of the house. They requested muffins. With a smile of heavenly sweetness tinged with regret, I replied that Saturday was our muffin day: Saturday, muffins; Tuesday, crumpets; Thursday, scones; and Friday, tea-cakes. This inspiration sprang into being full grown, like Pallas from the brain of Zeus. While they were regretting

that they had come on a plain bread-and-
butter day, I retired to the kitchen and
made out a bill for presentation to the
oldest man of the party.

	s.	*d.*
Nine teas	3	6
Cream		3
Bread and butter	1	0
Marmalade		6
	5	3

Feeling five and threepence to be an
absurdly small charge for five adult and
four infant teas, I destroyed this imme-
diately, and made out another, putting
each item fourpence more, and the bread
and butter at one and six. I also introduced ninepence for extra teas for the
children, who had had two mugs apiece,
very weak. This brought the total to six
shillings and tenpence, and I was beset
by a horrible temptation to add a shilling
or two for candles ; there was one young
man among the three who looked as if he
would have understood the joke.

The father of the family looked at the
bill, and remarked quizzically, "Bond
Street prices, eh ?"

"Bond Street service," said I, courtesy-ing demurely.

He paid it without flinching, and gave me sixpence for myself. I was very much afraid he would chuck me under the chin; they are always chucking barmaids under the chin in old English novels, but I have never seen it done in real life. As they strolled down to the gate, the second gentleman gave me another sixpence, and the nice young fellow gave me a shilling; he certainly had read the old English novels and remembered them, so I kept with the children. One of the ladies then asked if we sold flowers.

"Certainly," I replied.

"What do you ask for roses?"

"Fourpence apiece for the fine ones," I answered glibly, hoping it was enough, "thrippence for the smaller ones; sixpence for a bunch of sweet peas, tuppence apiece for buttonhole carnations."

Each of the ladies took some roses and mignonette, and the gentlemen, who did not care for carnations in the least, weakened when I approached modestly to pin them in their coats, *à la* barmaid.

At this moment one of the children began to tease for a canary.

"Have you one for sale?" inquired the fond mother.

"Certainly, madam." (I was prepared to sell the cottage by this time.)

"What do you ask for them?"

Rapid calculation on my part, excessively difficult without pencil and paper. A canary is three to five dollars in America, — that is, from twelve shillings to a pound; then at a venture, "From ten shillings to a guinea, madam, according to the quality of the bird."

"Would you like one for your birthday, Margaret, and do you think you can feed it and take quite good care of it?"

"Oh, yes, mamma!"

"Have you a cage?" to me inquiringly.

"Certainly, madam; it is not a new one, but I shall only charge you a shilling for it." (Impromptu plan: not knowing whether Mrs. Bobby had any cages, or if so where she kept them, to remove the canary in Mrs. Bobby's bedroom from the small wooden cage it inhabited, close the windows, and leave it at large in the apartment; then bring out the cage and sell it to the lady.)

"Very well, then, please select me a good singer for about twelve shillings; a very yellow one, please."

I did so. I had no difficulty about the color; but as the birds all stopped singing when I put my hand into the cages, I was somewhat at a loss to choose a really fine performer. I did my best, with the result that it turned out to be the mother of several fine families, but no vocalist, and the generous young man brought it back for an exchange some days afterwards.

The party finally mounted the char-a-bancs, just as I was about to offer the baby for twenty-five pounds, and dirt cheap at that; meanwhile, I gave the driver a cup of lukewarm tea, for which I refused absolutely to accept any remuneration.

I had cleared the tables before Mrs. Bobby returned, flushed and panting, with the guilty cow. Never shall I forget that good dame's astonishment, her mild deprecations, her smiles, — nay, her tears, — as she inspected my truly English account and received the silver.

	s.	d.
Nine teas	3	6
Cream		7
Bread and butter	1	6
Extra teas		9
Marmalade		6
Three tips	2	0
Four roses and mignonette	1	8
Three carnations		6
Canary	12	0
Cage	1	0
	24	0

I told her I regretted deeply putting down the marmalade so low as sixpence; but as they had not touched it, it did not matter so much, as the entire outlay for the entertainment had been only about a shilling. On that modest investment, I considered one pound three shillings a very fair sum to be earned by an inexperienced "licensed victualer" like myself, particularly as I am English only by adoption, and not by birth.

XXV

I essayed another nap after this exciting episode. I heard the gate open once

or twice, but a single stray customer, after
my hungry and generous horde, did not
stir my curiosity, and I sank into a re-
freshing slumber, dreaming that Willie
Beresford and I kept an English inn, and
that I was the barmaid. This blissful
vision had been of all too short duration
when I was awakened by Mrs. Bobby's
apologetic voice.

"It is too bad to disturb you, miss, but
I 've got to go and patch up the fence,
and smooth over the matter of the turnips
with Mrs. Gooch, who is that snorty I
don't know 'ow ever I can pacify her.
There is nothing for you to do, miss, only
if you 'll kindly keep an eye on the customer at the yew-tree table. He 's been
here for 'alf an hour, miss, and I think
more than likely he 's a foreigner, by his
actions, or may be he 's not quite right in
his 'ead, though 'armless. He has taken
four cups of tea, miss, and Billy saw him
turn two of them into the 'olly'ocks. He
has been feeding bread and butter to the
dog, and now the baby is on his knee,
playing with his fine gold watch. He
gave me a shilling and refused to take a

penny change ; but why does he stop so long, miss ? I can't help worriting over the silver cream jug that was my mother's."

Mrs. Bobby disappeared. I rose lazily, and approached the window to keep my promised eye on the mysterious customer. I lifted back the purple clematis to get a better view.

It was Willie Beresford! He looked up at my ejaculation of surprise, and, dropping the baby as if it had been a parcel, strode under the window.

I (gasping). How did you come here ?

He. By the usual methods, dear.

I. You should n't have come without asking. Where are all your fine promises ? What shall I do with you ? Do you know there is n't a hotel within four miles ?

He. That is nothing ; it was four hundred miles that I could n't endure. But give me a less grudging welcome than this, though I am like a starving dog that will snatch any morsel thrown to him ! It is really autumn, Penelope, or it will be in a few days. Say you are a little glad to see me.

(The sight of him so near, after my

weeks of loneliness, gave me a feeling so sudden, so sweet, and so vivid that it seemed to smite me first on the eyes, and then in the heart; and at the first note of his convincing voice Doubt picked up her trailing skirts and fled forever.)

I. Yes, if you must know it, I am glad to see you; so glad, indeed, that nothing in the world seems to matter so long as you are here.

He (striding a little nearer, and looking about involuntarily for a ladder). Penelope, do you know the penalty of saying such sweet things to me?

I. Perhaps it is because I know the penalty that I'm committing the offense. Besides, I feel safe in saying anything in this second-story window.

He. Don't pride yourself on your safety unless you wish to see me transformed into a nineteenth-century Romeo, to the detriment of Mrs. Bobby's vines. I can look at you forever, dear, in your pink gown and your purple frame, unless I can do better. Won't you come down?

I. I like it very much up here.

He. You would like it very much down

here, after a little. So you did n't "paint me out," after all?

I. No; on the contrary, I painted you in, to every twig and flower, every hill and meadow, every sunrise and every sunset.

He. You *must* come down! The distance between Belvern and Aix when I was not sure that you loved me was nothing compared to having you in a second story when I know that you do. Come down, Pen! Pretty Pen!

I. Suppose we compromise. My sitting-room is just below; will you walk in and look at my sketches until I come? You need n't ring; the bell is overgrown with honeysuckle and there is no one to answer it; it might almost be an American hotel, but it is, Arcadia!

He. It is Paradise; and alas! here comes the serpent!

I. It is n't a serpent; it is the kindest landlady in England.— Mrs. Bobby, this gentleman is a dear friend of mine from America. Mr. Beresford, this is Mrs. Bobby, the most comfortable hostess in the world, and the owner of the cottage, the canaries, the tea-tables, and the baby.

— The reason Mr. Beresford was so thirsty, Mrs. Bobby, was that he had walked here from Great Belvern, so we must give him some supper before he returns.

Mrs. B. Certainly, miss, he shall have the best in the 'ouse, you can depend upon that.

He. Don't let me interfere with your usual arrangements. I am not hungry — for food; I shall do very well until I get back to the hotel.

I. Indeed you will not, sir! Billy shall pull some tomatoes and lettuce, Tommy shall milk the cow, and Mrs. Bobby shall make you a savory omelet that Delmonico might envy. Hark! Is that our fowl cackling? It is, — at half past six! She heard me mention omelet, and she must be calling, " Now I lay me down to sleep."

.   .   .   .

But all that is many days ago, and there are no more experiences to relate at present. We are making history very fast, Willie Beresford and I, but much of it is sacred history, and so I cannot chronicle it for any one's amusement.

Mrs. Beresford is here, or at least she is in Great Belvern, a few miles distant. I am not painting, these latter days. I have turned the artist side of my nature to the wall just for a bit, and the woman side is having full play. I do not know what the world will think about it, if it stops to think at all, but I feel as if I were "right side out" for the first time in my life; and when I take up my brushes again, I shall have a new world within from which to paint, — yes, and a new world without.

Good-by, dear Belvern! Autumn and winter may come into my life, but whenever I think of you it will be summer-time in my heart. I shall hear the tinkle of the belled sheep on your hillsides ; inhale the fragrance of the flowering vine that climbed in at my cottage window; relive in memory the days when Love and I first walked together, hand in hand. Dear days of happy idleness ; of dreaming dreams and seeing visions ; of morning walks over the hills ; of "bread and cheese and kisses" at noon, with kind Mrs. Bobby hovering like a plump guardian angel over

the simple feast; afternoon tea under the
friendly shade of the yew-tree, and part-
ing at the wicket gate. I can see him
pass the clock tower, the little green-grocer
shop, the old stocks, the green pump;
then he is at the turn of the road where
the stone wall and the hawthorn hedge
will presently hide him from my view. I
fly up to my window, push back the vines,
catch his last wave of the hand. I would
call him back, if I dared; but it would be
no easier to let him go the second time,
and there is always to-morrow. Thank
God for to-morrow! And if there should be
no to-morrow? Then thank God for to-
day! And so good-by again, dear Belvern!
It was in the lap of your lovely hills that
Penelope first knew *das irdische Glück;*
that she first loved, first lived; forgot
how to be artist, in remembering how to
be woman.